COURTROOMS, CARTRIDGES, and CAMPFIRES

LAWYERING ON THE LAST FRONTIER—ALASKA

*To sue and Bill
with best Wishes
Wayne Anthony Ross*

Wayne Anthony Ross, B.S, J.D

PO Box 221974 Anchorage, Alaska 99522-1974
books@publicationconsultants.com—www.publicationconsultants.com

ISBN 978-1-59433-298-2
eBook SBN 978-1-59433-299-9
Library of Congress Catalog Card Number: 2012940467

Manufactured in the United States of America.

This book is dedicated to Barbara,
who chose to share a life with me in Alaska, far from anyone she knew.
And, I am forever grateful.
Anchorage, Alaska March, 2012.

Chapter 1
The Basketball Star

How does a kid from the South Side of Milwaukee end up as an attorney in Anchorage, Alaska?

In my case, it was simply because I couldn't play basketball.

I wasn't very good at baseball either.

In fact, as a kid I wasn't very good at any organized team sports. My lack of skill in sports, however, didn't stop me from trying. And my trying caused me some problems and a lot of embarrassment.

Most kids on Milwaukee's South Side in the 1940s and 1950s were Catholic. Of course, if there were kids on the South Side who weren't Catholic, I didn't know them. That's because Catholic parents didn't let their Catholic kids play with non-Catholic kids.

I did have a buddy who was Lutheran, but he lived next door. My folks apparently realized they couldn't stop me from playing with any kid who lived next door. They probably eased their consciences by reasoning that Lutherans were pretty close to being Catholic and Lutherans would still be Catholic if they hadn't been led astray, some years earlier, by a Catholic named Martin Luther. So it was OK for me to play with that Lutheran kid from next door. My folks probably secretly hoped that I'd convert the next-door kid back to Catholicism, right after I fulfilled their greatest hope … that I'd become a priest.

Like most other Catholic kids on Milwaukee's South Side, I attended a Catholic grade school. Such schools had basketball and baseball teams that played each other in what was known as, if I recall, the Catholic Conference.

I signed up for basketball. The coach was one of our parish priests, Father Nuedling. I was about five foot nothing tall, and so skinny if I stood sideways in a room, nobody knew I was there. Father Nuedling was interested in having Saint Rita's, his parish, field the winning Catholic Conference team. So Father did his very best to play the good players and avoid putting the bad players in a game.

Since I wasn't a good player, I didn't get to play much. Since I was, in fact, a very bad player, I usually sat on the bench until our team was about forty points ahead. Only when the game's outcome was not really in doubt would the bad players like me get to play.

My older sister, Kay, was dating the star center for the Marquette University basketball team. Kay wanted to bring her date to see her little brother play basketball. I didn't want her to come. I especially did not want her to bring her date. After all, what fun could it have been for my sister or her date, a big-shot basketball player, to watch me sit on the bench the whole game? And what fun could it be for me to know they were watching me sit on the bench?

Despite my continued protestations, however, Kay and her boyfriend showed up at one of my games. While I warmed the bench, somehow our team got forty points or more ahead. Then I heard Father Nuedling utter those long-sought magic words: "Ross, get in there!" Suddenly I was in the game! Determined to look good in front of my sister I managed to get ahold of the ball, skillfully dribbled it down the court, and quickly made my first basket! The crowd went wild!

Unfortunately, I had made the basket at the wrong end of the court. "Wrong-way" Corrigan had nothing on me!

That was the only basket I ever made in organized basketball. Father Nuedling took me aside and kindly suggested that perhaps organized sports were really not my forte. As a result, I gravitated to fishing, then to hunting, and finally to Alaska. But I'm getting ahead of my story …

Chapter 2
My Lineage Can't Be Traced To
The *Mayflower*

Some people can trace their lineage back to the *Mayflower*, or at least the Revolutionary War. I can trace mine back only three, maybe four generations. If any of my ancestors were in the Revolutionary War, they were probably Hessian troops supporting the British. That's because my genealogical research indicates that most of my ancestors, like the Hessians, came from Germany or Switzerland.

My father's grandfather-my great-grandfather-came from Germany in the second half of the nineteenth century. His name was John Meyerholtz and, according to family tradition, he settled first in Cairo, Illinois.

As my father told the story, John Meyerholtz lived with a Polish family in Cairo and to honor them he changed his name to Rogowsky. My mother told a somewhat different version of the story. According to Mom, shortly after John Meyerholtz arrived in the United States, he was walking down the streets of Cairo and decided that he needed a good American name. Seeing the name Rogowsky on a butcher shop, my great-grandfather thought that sounded like what he imagined was a good American name, and he chose it for his own.

Whatever version is correct, my grandfather Anton, and my father Raymond were Rogowskys until they changed the name to Ross in 1927.

John (Meyerholtz) Rogowsky married Amelia Gajewski and they had at least eight children.

One of them, my grandfather Anton, was born in LaCrosse, Wisconsin. While there Anton met my grandmother, Emma Kokta. Her father, Joseph Kokta, was a LaCrosse policeman. On my office wall is an old photograph of my great-grandfather Joseph in his LaCrosse police uniform. With his nightstick and walrus mustache, Joe Kokta looks like a guy you wouldn't have wanted to mess with.

My paternal grandparents, Anton and Emma, were married in 1900 and my father was born in 1903. Later Anton moved his family to Milwaukee where he went to work for Allis-Chalmers Manufacturing Company. Allis-Chalmers, in addition to making the orange tractors for which they were most famous, also manufactured steam turbine generators. My father always held that Anton, my grandfather, was a "trouble-shooter for Allis-Chalmers." Dad said his father was sent "all over the country," and to "every province in Canada and Mexico" to maintain and repair Allis Chalmers turbines.

This photo of my great-grandfather, Joseph Kokta, hangs on my office wall.

My mother's family, the Steiners, also came from Germany in the second half of the nineteenth century. Martin Steiner, my great-grandfather came to America in 1872. He married Maria Waldvogel, who also immigrated here that same year. Martin and Maria had thirteen children, one of whom died in infancy. My grandfather, Louis, was one of the twelve surviving kids.

Louis married Anna Ofenlock and they had four children, my mother Lillian Steiner being the youngest.

Dad and Mom often said it was a good thing my father had changed his name. According to my folks, ethnic Germans and ethnic Poles who lived on

Milwaukee's South Side in the early decades of the twentieth century did not get along very well. In fact, they did not get along at all. Had my father retained his Polish-sounding name, he and my mother-with her German background-would either not have met, or probably would have been discouraged by their friends if not their parents from having anything to do with one another. Certainly they would not have been able to court one another.

My father and mother, Ray and Lillian, were married in 1930 in Milwaukee during the start of the Depression and times were tough. I have a picture of my father's 1929 Chevrolet, taken before their marriage, with Mom in a summer dress leaning on the driver's door. Mom is squinting, and it is obviously a bright spring day. Dad often pointed at that picture proudly, and told how he sold his Chevrolet to buy my mom a diamond engagement ring.

My dad often pointed to this picture proudly, and told how he sold this 1929 Chevrolet to buy my mom (shown here) a diamond engagement ring.

Dad took his new bride to Chicago and managed an apartment building at 6812 Wayne Avenue during what was known as the "the gangster era." Dad told us numerous stories about those times.

On one occasion, according to Dad, my mom's mother was visiting Chicago from Milwaukee to see her newly married daughter and son-in-law. While everyone was out for dinner, someone burglarized my folks' apartment, stealing a cocktail ring my mother prized highly. After the burglary Anna Steiner wanted her daughter, Lillian, to come home to Milwaukee "where it is safe!"

On another occasion, my father was chased through the building by a drunken gangster who didn't like the fact that my dad was evicting him for failure to pay rent.

One day J. Edgar Hoover's FBI thought they had cornered John Dillinger and his gang in an apartment in my parents' neighborhood. After a violent shootout involving Thompson machine guns and other weapons, the FBI killed the residents of the apartment only to learn it wasn't Dillinger or his men. Instead, the deceased were several small-time Chicago thieves. Dad and several neighbors were taken on a tour of the shot-up apartment before the bodies were taken away. "One of the bodies was almost torn in half by that Thompson," my father would remember.

My favorite Chicago story was the one Dad would tell us about "Ruby." I've only met a few women named Ruby in my life, and each of them was impressive. I know the Ruby in Dad's story was. Before he died, Dad gave me the yellowed newspaper clippings he had saved from the Chicago papers of September 1932, describing how the police broke up a holdup gang. Some of the gang members, Ruby included, lived in the apartment building Dad managed.

Two guys and Ruby had rented an apartment from my father. "They were driving a big Pierce Arrow car" my father would say, "and they moved a lot of clothes and things into the apartment." Shortly thereafter, the two guys argued over the attentions of Ruby, and one guy got shot.

Under the headline "TWO GIRLS, FIVE MEN SEIZED AS BANDIT GANG" the story unfolded in the clippings Dad had kept:

> Two girls, a wounded man in a Rogers Park Hospital, and four other men were held by Rogers Park police today in what was said to be a roundup of a gang responsible for between 75 and 100 robberies. One of the girls, who gave the name of Miss Ruby Ward, 20, of 6812 Wayne Avenue, was said by Capt. Patrick Harding … to have been identified as the "bandit queen" who chauffeured the gang's automobile and acted as lookout for her alleged confederates while various holdups were in progress.

Another article, entitled "A NINE O'CLOCK GIRL GETS INTO FAST COMPANY" stated Ruby Ward used to live in Cleburne, Texas "

... which she claims was a nine o'clock town and pretty quiet in the day-time too." The article continued:

> So she went up to Fort Worth a few months ago. There she met a dudish fellow named Howard Hargraves. He looked like romance and Ruby decided that the thing to do then was to come to Chicago with him and help him in his business. Howard's business was sticking guns in people's ribs and making them give him the money in the cash register. Ruby, who is a stout blond girl with steady nerves, fitted in all right. Her friend and his business associates gave her a nice pistol with a little holster which she swung under her armpit with a pink ribbon.

As I said, Ruby Ward must have been some gal.

After the gang was arrested, police found stolen suits, dresses, jewelry, guns, and other things in the apartment the robbery gang had rented from Dad. Dad told how the police hauled the stolen goods out of the apartment for several hours but he doubted that any of those goods were returned to their lawful owners because "in those days, the Chicago police were almost as crooked as the criminals they were supposed to be apprehending."

After the police cleaned out the apartment Dad found a leather sap and a handful of pistol cartridges had been overlooked. I still have the sap and cartridges.

My older brother Don and my sister Kay were born in the 1930s. Eventually Dad and Mom moved back to Milwaukee. They bought a building lot in a subdivision called Mitchell Manor, once part of a large estate called Meadowmere, which had been the boyhood home of General William "Billy" Mitchell[1]. My folks built a yellow Cape Cod house at 2369 South 57th Street. Thus, like Billy Mitchell's, my boyhood home was also on the Meadowmere land.

Shortly after my folks moved into their new house, there was a knock at the door one evening. When my dad opened the front door a man and a woman, carrying a 12-foot ladder between them, walked in. Without saying one word, the couple carrying the ladder maneuvered their way through the house and walked out the back door. That was how my folks initially met the Piaseckis, their first friends in the neighborhood. Later

---

[1] Billy Mitchell, an army general, was a leading advocate of air power, who was court-martialed for what were, at the time, his extremist views. His views of air power were later vindicated by the American experiences of World War Two.

Bertha Piasecki made a beautiful birthday cake for Dad. When Dad cut into the cake, it was filled with old rags. Remember, this was before television. As Dad put it, "In those days we had to make our own entertainment."

Eventually, my father arranged for a State Historical Marker to be erected in a little park across the street from our home, officially recognizing the area as "Meadowmere-The Boyhood Home of Billy Mitchell[2]."

---

[2] After my father died, I came across a letter written to him by General Mitchell's sister over sixty years ago. In it she described Meadowmere and her life there. She wrote:

> Meadowmere built in about 1884 by John L. and Harriet Danforth Mitchell had 600 acres of woods and fields surrounding the house. A pretty lake with water fall was not far from the big home. The large racing stables with 28 box stalls were a mile to the west of the house on the Hawley Road. Between them and the house was the fine 3/4 mile race tract (sic). In fact the only privately owned race tract of that size in the U.S. at that time. The farm buildings and stable for the carriage horses were near the house. North of the house an artesian well formed a round pool and shot a stream 8 feet high in the air. During the building of this great house artists and craftsmen were brought west from New York to do wood carving and frescoes on the walls. The handsome inlaid floors were covered with the finest ori- ental rugs. There were beautiful paintings on the walls. My father being one of the best judges of pictures in this country. People came from far and wide to see the big porcelain bath tubs on the second floor. (If they are still there notice the funny old handles). At Thanksgiving and Xmas time we had large gatherings, often seating from 30 to 40 people in the dining room at such times. There were always big fires in the fire places in the hall and living room where we gathered. Being a musical family I remembered we had 3 pianos in the house for several years, besides many other instruments.

> As my father loved books and was a great reader he accumulated a beautiful library numbering several thousand books. Not only the library and book room were filled with rare editions, but also the large billiard room on the third floor. To me the most attractive room in the house was my mother's bed room over the library. The bamboo woodwork and inlaid furniture were brought from China.

> I have part of her furniture now in my own bed room at Little Meadowmere. It is inlaid with gold and mother-of-pearl butterflies and birds. Although I am very glad not to have the care of that beautiful big house I loved every bit of it and although my brother 'Billy Mitchell' and my sisters got most of the furniture I have so much that I prize from the old place. The attic was perhaps my most favorite spot. Two small rooms were always kept locked, and so became very mysterious. One contained old prints and paintings, the other beautiful glass and china which had belonged to my grandmother, Mrs. Alexander Mitchell . There were trunks full of treasures, but the thing I liked best were the rows of birds up high on shelves in a dark corner. They were a collections of birds my brother Billy shot himself at Meadowmere before he was twelve years old. Dr. Carl Akeley, who later became a famous naturalist and was at that time with our own (Milwaukee's) public museum, helped my brother stuff and mount over 100 specimens. They are now at the Public Museum and can be seen there.

The canoes he used in the little lake and on camping trips as a boy are at the museum also, and many other possessions of his. As a small child my brother had a little black pony named Topsy and I believe there are still neighbors who remember seeing him tearing down the roads and through the woods. He was always a fearless, inquisitive child. Many people smiled at the idea of my father being a farmer but no part of life afforded him greater satisfaction or pleasure than living in the country with plenty of fresh air, broad acres and shady woods. He bred fine trotting horses and had a beautiful herd of Jersey cows. I remember the large St. Bernard dogs and my mother told me we kept six of them for quite a long time. They resembled the stone dogs that still guard the front entrance today.

Many distinguished people were entertained at Meadowmere. General Douglass MacArthur (sic) came with his parents to visit. General Bragg, General Black, Colonel Pabst, The Vilas', Spooners and Senator Stephenson were frequent visitors.

Mr. Mitchell, a student all his life, gave freely of his time and means to the advancement of education. For many years he bought school books for all the children of Milwaukee whose parents were too poor to pay for them. He helped to establish the College of Agriculture at Madison. In 1891 he gave 20 scholarships a year to farm boys. He gave the land where the State Fair is now held and was instrumental in moving the Fair from Madison to Milwaukee. He helped establish the first water works for Milwaukee. He established the first fish hatchery in the state. Always being public spirited and generous, he gave Mitchell Park to the City of Milwaukee. Also the land where the Public Library and Museum now stand. All the land south of the tracts at Soldiers Home was donated by him for the veterans of the Civil War.

In 1890 he was elected a representative to Congress; in 1892 he was elected United States Senator from Wisconsin. He was widely quoted throughout the country for a letter written to Judge Carpenter just before the outbreak of the Spanish American War in which he wrote: "There are some things worse than war. There are some things better than money."

He traveled a great deal and spoke five languages fluently, but I know his happiest days were spent at Meadowmere. My mother and father had nine children but I happened to be the only one born at Meadowmere, and for that reason perhaps cared for it more than the others.

There is a great deal more I might tell you about my beautiful brave mother who lived on at Meadowmere for 19 years after my father's death but I shall end with a quotation from a speech of his to the Agricultural Society.

Fortunate is he who leads a life of rural quietude, crowned with its abundant fruits, remote from the city's struggling throng, fired with delusive ambitions. The city may have its amusements, its feverish successes, but the country is the place to be serenely happy in.

Harriet Mitchell Fladoes

December 12, 1947"

Chapter 3
Early Memories

My mother used to tell me the old western program *Gunsmoke* was being broadcast on the car radio as Dad drove Mom to the hospital to give birth to me. Mom said that some poor fellow was about to be hanged, and she never did find out whether or not he survived. Maybe that's the reason why I always liked cowboys and why I've always been against the death penalty.

I believe my first conscious memory was VJ Day. I have dim memories of walking along the bluff overlooking Lake Michigan in downtown Milwaukee with a lot of happy people, sunshine, and flags. I would have been about two and a half years old.

Another early memory was the Great Blizzard of 1947 when I was four years old. That snow storm (January 29-30, 1947) was the greatest storm in Milwaukee history. According to the *Milwaukee Journal-Sentinel* "that whopper produced an estimated 9.6 billion pounds of snow (somebody actually figured it out) that rose 18 inches and drifted mightily."

Snowfalls of 18 inches don't seem excessive. The Great Blizzard of 1947 in Milwaukee, however, had winds gusting to 60 miles per hour for hours, building up drifts 10 to 15 feet high. Snow on Milwaukee's National Avenue was 5 to 6 feet deep. Nobody went to work for three days.

After the storm, I walked with my Dad and my brother to my aunt's house. Aunt Bernice lived only several houses away but she could not get out of her doors because of the snowdrifts. Dad carried an extension ladder and put it up to her second-story attic window. Aunt Bernice then climbed out the window, down the ladder, and went with us to our home until my older brother, my dad, and my uncle Phil Thullen could shovel away the drifts covering the doors of her house. The whole event was a big adventure to a little kid like me.

———

Aunt Bernice lived next to Mr. and Mrs. Dahmer. The Dahmers were teachers. They had two kids, Lionel and Eunice. Lionel and Eunice were both older than I was.

I always thought it must have been tough on kids in the 1940s and 1950s, or any other time for that matter, to be named Lionel and Eunice.

I have only a few memories of Eunice Dahmer. One was of her bike. It was a girl's bike, of course, with a basket on the front and a guard, called a skirt guard, over the rear wheel to keep skirts from getting tangled in the spokes. Eunice would wear a straw hat with ribbons down the back when she rode that bike.

I remember only two things about Lionel Dahmer: first, he was the only kid in the neighborhood whose folks would let him set up his electric train outside and run it in the garden.

The other thing was that Lionel had a dummy which he dressed in old clothes. Lionel then ran a thin rope across the street in front of his house and hung the dummy from the rope. The dummy was somehow rigged so when Lionel pulled a string, the dummy sailed out into the middle of the road like it was some guy running across the street. Lionel set it up at night in the summer and when a car came down our street, Lionel turned the dummy loose. To the driver, all of a sudden it appeared some guy had jumped out in front of the car. There'd be a loud squeal of brakes. Sometimes the car hit the dummy and sometimes not, but I am sure every driver was almost scared to death.

Lionel grew up and became the father of Jeffrey Dahmer, Milwaukee's infamous serial murderer.

———

Dad woke me very early one morning. We drove down to Milwaukee's Lake Front to see the Ringling Brothers-Barnum & Bailey circus train arrive. I am told that occasion was the last year that circus operated under "The Big Top" as the large tent was called. I saw the tent and its poles being raised by elephants. My most vivid memory is of the fellows whose job it was to pound in the tent stakes. Five or six of them, holding long-handled wooden mallets, stood in a circle around the tent stake. In perfect synchronization, those fellows hit that stake one after another, round and round the circle, until the stake was deemed deep enough in the ground to hold the guy ropes for the big tent. A day or so later, Dad took me to see the show under The Big Top. My favorite act was where about twenty-seven clowns all managed to get out of one little car.

———

When my younger sister, Carol Ann, was born, Mom was quite ill. My dad hired an old lady, Mrs. Harding, to help Mom while Carol Ann was placed in the care of the Daughters of Charity until Mom was well enough for the baby to come home. One nun, Sister Mary Williams, took special care of my sister and, as a result, became a great friend of our family. At least one Sunday afternoon every few months, for years, Dad and Mom would take Carol Ann and me to visit Sister Mary Williams at Saint Vincent's Orphanage, which the sisters operated on Milwaukee's South Side.

There aren't many orphanages these days. Now kids are put in foster homes.

After she came home, Carol Ann and I became inseparable. Today, she's a liberal San Francisco area artist who votes Democrat, so we avoid talking politics!

———

My home life was typical of the late 1940s and 1950s. We lived in a quiet neighborhood. Dad was the breadwinner working as a sales agent for the Prudential Insurance Company, while Mom was the housewife staying home and taking care of the kids.

My folks entertained a lot for birthdays, or first communions, or any other reason. Sometimes it was friends; other times it was relatives. If the weather was nice, Dad would set up some long tables in the backyard and serve dinner picnic-style. If it was winter, or cold, or rainy, Mom served everyone at the dining room table.

When my folks went out of town for a sales meeting or for a convention, my dad's other sister, Aunt Sylvia, and her husband, Uncle Homer Gilman, stayed with us. Aunt Sylvia was a good cook and somewhere she read about a new type of meal called "pizza pie." She had never seen one. None of us had. But Aunt Sylvia read what she could find out about pizza pie, and decided she had to try making one. No one ever told her pizza was supposed to be served on a flat crust. So Aunt Sylvia got out one of Mom's pie pans and made a pizza pie. It looked like any other pie but it was filled with just about everything ever put on a pizza, and it was about two inches thick! It was wonderful! To this day, I've never had a pizza that could compare with Aunt Sylvia's.

I really enjoyed when the relatives came. Mom's sister, my aunt Rose, was married to a man named Phil Goetz. Uncle Phil Goetz smoked cigars and when they got down to an inch or two in length, without using his hands Uncle Phil could reverse that cigar in his mouth so that the lit end was inside his mouth. He'd then smoke for a while with the lighted end in his mouth. Then he'd reverse it again, without using his hands, so the lighted end was once again outside his lips. Uncle Phil Goetz was a talented guy.

My mom's other sister was Irmgard. Aunt Irmgard's husband, George Burmeister, was part owner of a hardware store. Uncle George was a big, quiet man who enjoyed the outdoors. Irmgard and my mom could talk for hours on end. They thoroughly enjoyed one another's company and were as close as any sisters could be. After a while, Uncle George would get bored, and go and sit in the car to let Aunt Irmgard know he was ready to go. Aunt Irmgard didn't care; she and Mom were enjoying themselves. Sometimes Uncle George sat in the car for several hours before Aunt Irmgard decided to leave.

Mom's only brother was Louis Steiner. "Uncle Louie" too was a quiet guy. His wife, my aunt Esther, was just the opposite. At every gathering, Aunt Esther would sit down and play the piano and sing. She was always the loudest one present, and everyone considered her the life of the party.

Once a month, Mom even had a few lady friends who came in the evening to play canasta.

We had a very happy life on South 57th Street. Both of my parents loved one another and really looked after each other and us kids.

———

Christmas was a special time because my Dad was a personal friend of Santa Claus. As a result Santa Claus would actually visit our house on Christmas Eve! Santa came in the front door with a hearty "Ho! Ho! Ho!", and said a few words to Dad and Mom as if seeing old friends, and then he talked to each of us kids. Santa seemed to know if we had been naughty or nice (of course I had *always* been nice) and he seemed to know just what each of us had been up to. Then he'd have to leave to visit the other kids around the world, most of whom did not have a father who actually knew Santa Claus. In those early years, I actually felt sorry for those kids because Santa only came to visit them at night, sliding down their chimney while they were asleep, while Santa came to see us first, in person, red suit, beard and all!

As we got a little older, the kids at school would argue over whether or not Santa Claus actually existed. When I proudly pointed out my Dad was a personal friend of Santa Claus, and Santa actually came to our house each year, they were quite impressed.

I finally realized the real Santa didn't actually come to our house the Christmas after my dad's good friend, Charlie Burbach died. Mr. Burbach had been our Santa for years, and my folks had to find somebody else to do the job. That last year of my innocence, after Santa had left our house, I peeked out the window to try and get a glimpse of his sleigh. Instead of flying off in a sleigh, Santa drove off in a copper-colored Ford just like the one owned by Mr. McCarthy, a man who lived across our alley.

———

The other two holidays we really enjoyed were Fourth of July and Halloween.

For several weeks before the Fourth of July, we kids would get prepared. Mom and Dad bought rolls of colored crepe paper, and we guys decorated our bikes, weaving the bright paper between the spokes so the wheels looked solid red, white and blue. We then started on the handle bars, covering them with crepe paper also, liberally fastened down with scotch tape. We festooned the bikes with American flags.

My sisters and their friends decorated up their baby buggies. (The old joke is: She: "Do you know how to drive a baby buggy?" He: "Sure. Tickle its feet.")

When the big holiday arrived, it was the sound of fireworks going off around the neighborhood that woke us up. In our town, such private detonations were illegal, and we kids never had any firecrackers. Each year Dad told the story of the only time he ever got arrested. It was for shooting off an illegal firecracker just after he and Mom were married. We always loved to hear that story because Dad was the only person we knew who had ever been arrested.

At half past nine in the morning, all the kids in town gathered near the Allis Chalmers plant for the big parade that started at 10 AM. The parade route ran along our main street, Greenfield Avenue, for sixteen or eighteen blocks. All the kids marched in the parade. (Thinking back, I wonder who was left to watch it?) Of course the high school bands, the Shriners, the Knights of Columbus, and the World War I vets marched too. There were always horses, and the city proudly displayed its new fire engines and street sweepers by running them in the parade. There was always an open topped-car of some kind for a few of the surviving Civil War veterans who rode and waved to the crowd.

The parade ended at the State Fair Park where the VFW and the Rotarians would give every kid an American flag and a box of Cracker Jack.

After cotton candy and hot dogs, there would be a parade of the decorated bikes and baby buggies at the fairgrounds, and prizes were awarded. Mom and Dad gave each of us fifty cents so the we could ride five of the carnival rides. The scariest one, the Big Dipper, we'd save until last. That was the one we always got sick and threw up on, and after all, we didn't want to be sick before we had spent all of our money.

Then we'd go home. Dad would trundle out the charcoal grill (we were one of the first in the neighborhood to have one) and cook hamburgers and bratwurst over the coals. Afterwards, he'd give us kids extendable metal forks and a bag of marshmallows, and it was our turn to use the grill.

Visiting with my older brother at Fort Eustis, Virginia during the Korean War (1952). (Back row center) my brother Don - (Back row right) my sister Kay - (Front row, left to right) my mom, sister Carol, and the author.

After dark, we'd go back to the State Fair Park, or to Jackson Park, for the big fireworks display put on by the County Park Commission.

Halloween was another great event. My father had a good friend-my father actually had a lot of good friends-who owned the local grocery store. Frank Gerencier liked kids and was a generous man. On Halloween Day, he'd block off the store's parking lot and have a bunch of bleachers set up, along with a big movie screen. We kids dressed up in costumes and headed down to that parking lot just after it got dark. We each were given a bag of candy and, of course that old stand-by, a box of Cracker Jack, and we'd settle on to the bleachers for some movies. There would be a number of cartoons and an Abbott and Costello or Three Stooges film. During the intermissions, there'd be clowns or magicians, and an animal act or two.

Then came the big parade down Lincoln Avenue, led by a couple of police cars or fire trucks. As each kid got near his or her home, they'd leave the parade, stand on the curb watching the rest of it go by, and then trudge off home. We all loved Halloween and we all loved Mr. Gerencier.

———

During the Korean War, my older brother, Don, was drafted. He underwent basic training at Fort Eustis, Virginia. Dad and Mom decided that we should drive to Virginia to see Don and, at the same time, tour the East Coast. So we piled into Dad's new 1951 burgundy-colored Chevrolet Deluxe and headed east. We visited the Ford Museum at Dearborn, Niagara Falls, and even went to New York City, where we stayed at the old Holland Hotel.

One day we went to Coney Island. Somehow Dad persuaded me to go up in the Parachute Drop. I got into a small canvas seat and was taken up 250 feet in the air and then dropped. Before I could hit the ground with a splat, the parachute opened and I drifted to a smooth landing. During the descent before the parachute opened, however, I was convinced that I was going to die at eight years old!

I have been terrified of heights ever since.

We went to the Yorktown Battlefield, visited Washington DC, and saw the Capitol, Lincoln Memorial, Bureau of Engraving and everything else a tourist should see.

Farther south, we rode a ferry from Newport News to Norfolk. I had never been on such a boat and explored it as much as a kid of eight could get away with. When I got to the back of the boat, I noticed it was full of Negroes. One Negro lady told me, most kindly, that the stern section of the boat was for Negroes and that since I was a White Boy, I needed to go back to the bow section. That was my first experience with segregation. I talked it over with my folks and we agreed that segregation wasn't fair, and that we were glad we lived in Milwaukee where anyone could ride the Lake Michigan ferry The Milwaukee Clipper and sit anywhere they wanted to.

At Fort Eustis we were told that we would not be allowed to see my brother. Apparently someone in his unit had misplaced "something" and the entire unit had been placed on restriction until the missing "something" was located. My mother was heartbroken and my father was angry, one of the few times I ever saw him that way. My father was not a guy who was going to drive several thousand miles to see his boy, and then not be able to see him. So Dad went to see the base commander, or as Dad put it, "I went to see the general!" Dad never told us just what it was that he said to the general but after Dad and the general had their little chat, we all enjoyed a good visit with my brother. Then we drove back to Wisconsin.

Don was shipped to Korea and was gone for about a year. When he came back, he brought wonderful souvenirs such as bamboo fishing rods, knives, little ceramic figures, and even Korean 78 RPM phonograph records so we all could listen to Korean songs. Don's return was an almost magical time.

———

My sister Kay, more than forty years ago, wrote a letter much like the one General Billy Mitchell's sister, Harriet Fladoes, had written to my dad about her memories living at Meadowmere. Kay's letter, however, contained her memories of living on South 57th Street. I came across Kay's letter after I had written this chapter and it was interesting to note that many of the things I wrote about were things Kay had remembered as well. Kay wrote:

Sat. Aug 16, 1969

…Remember the formal gardens dad and mom made in our back-yard at 2369. It was horseshoe shaped, with mother's beloved poplar trees in back, and then glorious flowers, including rose bushes near the garage door, and 'hens and chicks' plants on rocks near Steffans' yard, and little clustered blue and white flowers edging the flower beds. Chives grew near the backdoor, sometimes near daffodils and some-times tulips. For a while the green tiled back porch had morning glories growing up strings, and once someone fell into them and broke them down all of the strings. The upstairs porch (had) a red metal floor that got very hot, and a railing that mother had to continually caution us to not hang over or lean on. There were ferns and beautiful lilies of the valley between the garages, and ants helped open the big red flowers beneath the curtained garage window. Dad grew a glorious magnolia by keeping it covered with a burlap lean-to in winter. Remember the Baptismal, Confirmation, and Communion parties the folks had for us, serving about 30 relatives a big hot meal and drinks, often out in the backyard on long church tables, and folding chairs. Our room (the girls' room) had blue and white lacy wallpaper … and the cute cupola. And Wayne and Don had the bunk beds and boyish brown decor. Mother would get out the out-of-season clothes as they came back in season (from the little attic door) and try all the clothes on us, and lengthen dresses, and take us shopping for more, or sometimes get boxes full from Aunt Irmgard that Dorothy (her daughter - our cousin) outgrew. I recall the coalbin in the basement and coal was delivered down a chute thru the (basement) window. And recall the fruit cellar, for a while our bomb shelter. Also planting and weeding the victory garden, and the fire that spread while burning dry cornstalks.

The Mitchell Manor Garden Club met once a year at our home. Mother had her afternoon, and her evening club. They cackled and played cards (Canasta) in the evening, and mended socks in the afternoon every few weeks. Mom talked on the phone to Aunt Irmgard almost every day, and said things in German when she didn't want us to understand. She bathed Wayne, and later Carol, in the black tiled kitchen sink, and sang 'Deedle Deedle Dumpling' and 'Little Brown Jug How I Love Thee' to you daily as she bathed, powdered, oiled and kissed and kissed you, always 'back of the necks' and even baby's bottoms. When we ate outside, we handed food and dishes in thru the back (kitchen) window. Dad often bought a pint of ice cream home for us after (work at night), and got us down from bed for some, or homemade pop corn. Sliding down the bannister was forbidden. Mother made a beautiful white bedspread with red and white checkered trip for the downstairs bedroom, and we were brought trays there, with lace doilies when we were sick. She kept the dining room china cabinets sparkling. Dad was so handy he always fixed everything and I recall some one of us always (taking something that was broken to him and) saying 'Daddy Fix!' He painted the outside, shoveled the big snows, removed old wallpaper, and after about 16 years there, they bought us our new home... .There were the Thursday afternoon picnics in Jackson Park with Aunt Rose, Aunt Irmgard, and all our cousins, and I recall the happy shouts as dad came across the park to join us after work.

Mom taught me always to have balanced meals... meat, potatoes, vegetables, salad and milk. Remember her fruit salad, a pineapple ring (in green jell-O) with half a banana standing (in the center) like a candle, and a cherry on top. The Cold Spot refrigerator. The back porch Dad built. Our baseball diamond where Huber's house was later built. Mom's and Dad's fabulous Christmas decorating indoors and out. The 'real' Santa Clauses that came to our house ...

Much love,
Kay Ross Reul"

Chapter 4
Early Schooling

I started formal schooling earlier than most kids. I can remember my folks taking me somewhere where I had to take a test to see if I was smart enough for kindergarten. The test had line-drawn pictures on it. One question had four bunnies. Three bunnies faced right, and one bunny faced left. It is a good thing I didn't have to say whether the bunnies were facing right or facing left, because I still didn't know which hand was my right one and which one was my left. Instead, I was supposed to look at the four bunnies and say which one was different. The questions got trickier and trickier. The next box had all four bunnies facing the same direction, but one had a bow and the other three did not. Again "Which one is different?" I think I also had to know my colors.

I must have done alright because that fall I attended Longfellow Kindergarten. Since I started formal schooling early, throughout my grade school and high school years I was always younger than the others in my classes. That was a bummer later, when I discovered girls because every girl in my class was "too old" for me. Actually (and more accurately), they thought I was "too young" for them (and they were right!).

Miss Lyons was my kindergarten teacher. She was in her late twenties or early thirties and I thought she was beautiful. Kind of like the good fairy in the Wizard of Oz. There was a second teacher, too, who was really old. She must have been fifty! I don't remember her name. She was nice too, but not as nice as Miss Lyons.

Kindergarten was cool. We had stories read to us, and got to play with building blocks. The most fun was playing with modeling clay. I got really good making bunnies and birds' nests. Other kids must have been good at that too, because I cannot recall anyone in my kindergarten ever flunking clay class.

The next year I started grade school at Saint Rita's Catholic School. Saint Rita's was on South 60th Street and we lived on South 57th Street so we had about a four-block walk. As I tell my kids, it was uphill each way.

Actually it was an easy walk except when the winter wind came whipping off Lake Michigan and the temperature was zero or below. There were actually times each winter when we had to walk backwards to school because if we faced the wind, it was blowing so hard we couldn't breathe.

Although there were a couple of lay teachers at Saint Rita's, most of our teachers were nuns. I liked the nuns I had as teachers, and they seemed to like me too. Some of the other classes, however, had some pretty tough nuns. Those tough ones carried rulers and cracked students' knuckles with them. If they tried that nowadays, those nuns would be carted off to jail for child abuse!

I can recall one traumatic incident in first grade. I had a hand-painted cast-lead Indian chief on my desk and I suppose I was playing with the chief rather than paying attention. Sister Janice came by and the chief suddenly rose in the air like the ascension of Jesus Christ into heaven. I never saw the chief again and it was fully forty years later when I found, and bought another like him in an antique shop in San Pedro.

I also remember feeling like a hero for almost an hour once when a white rat got out of his cage and went running down the hallway. The girls were yelling and screaming and fainting, and I chased down the rat, caught him, and returned him to his cage. During that adventure, the rat bit me twice, and the school nurse painted the bites with Mercurochrome. The nun called me "brave." Some of the guys, however, called me "dumb."

One of the worst times was recess. Generally the guys played baseball while the girls played jacks or other girls' games. Two of the biggest guys in class would be chosen team captains. Then someone tossed one of them a baseball bat, which the team captain caught in one hand. The other captain would put his hand higher up the bat, and the first guy would then move his hand above that of the second guy, alternating until the fellow whose hand reached the top of the bat got first choice in picking somebody for his team. The second captain then chose next, and then back and forth until everybody who wanted to play was on a team. At least everybody but me. Usually I was the last guy picked. I can remember "You take Ross." "No! You take Ross." Or sometimes it was "Awww ... Do we have to take Ross?" Much of the time, however, I would forgo the pleasure of having guys fight over me and, instead, I'd join the other nerdy guys playing marbles. I never got very good at baseball but I sure got pretty good at marbles.

Some guys would "flip" baseball cards with others, calling "odds" or "evens." When the cards hit the ground and both were face up, the guy calling evens took his baseball card back and he also got to keep the other guy's card. If, however, he called evens and the cards hit the ground, one face up and one face down, the other guy got to keep the cards. I never got bubble gum much so I never had too many baseball cards. I certainly didn't have enough to risk in a high-stake game of flipping.

One of my buddies was a little guy named Michael Turk. I was his buddy because I'd walk him home and protect him from other guys who liked to pick on him. He was my buddy because he had a huge trunk of comic books in his basement and he'd usually let me borrow two or three at a time. When I brought the borrowed ones back, he'd loan me a couple more. If I had that trunk of comic books now, I could probably get $50,000 for what was in there.

Michael Turk's father drove a bronze Buick with a "Joe Must Go!" bumper sticker. Mr. Turk was one of the few voters in Wisconsin who didn't like our U.S. senator, Joe McCarthy. Mr. Turk was a duck hunter and he'd bring ducks home now and then. That was my first exposure to the hunting culture. At the time, I wondered how anybody could shoot a duck ... they seemed so cute. And weren't my favorite comic characters, Uncle Scrooge and Donald, both ducks?

Another buddy was Tom Manning. We got to know each other in second grade and have been friends ever since. Over the years we've had a lot of great adventures together. Tom-his mother called him Tommy-had a terrific collection of toy soldiers and we spent many hours playing with them. On several summer mornings, we'd get up at 6 AM, ride our bikes 25 miles from West Allis to Waterford, have breakfast with another class-mate, and then ride our bikes back home in time for lunch. The roads we peddled on back then are now expressways. Nowadays, if a kid tried to ride a bike on the roads we used, he'd probably get run over or issued a traffic citation.

Chapter 5
The Balloon Man

The Balloon Man and his wife lived across the alley and up the block from our house. The Balloon Man and his wife, whose real names were Mr. and Mrs. Jerabek, had a son about my age named Ricky. The Balloon Man and his wife always called him Richard. We never knew why.

The Balloon Man and his wife lived in a two-story brick house covered with ivy. There was so much ivy that no one knew The Balloon Man lived in a brick house. Then one year some men came and trimmed the ivy back and we kids were able to see the brick on Ricky's house for the first time.

The Balloon Man's house was always cool inside. I guess the ivy helped keep it that way. On hot summer days we kids always enjoyed being invited into the cool of The Balloon Man's house.

The Balloon Man and his wife liked kids. We'd spend many long summer afternoons at their house, playing Monopoly or Pollyanna or other board games, and we always knew eventually The Balloon Man's wife would bring us a big pitcher of Kool-Aid and some cookies or popcorn. She'd serve the Kool-Aid in aluminum glasses filled with ice cubes. The aluminum glasses would sweat and we'd draw funny faces in the moisture on the outside of the glasses.

Behind their house near the alley, The Balloon Man and his wife had a huge elm tree with branches shading the entire backyard. We'd play marbles in the dirt beneath that tree, or we'd dig in the sandbox The Balloon Man had built for us.

The Balloon Man and his wife always had a lot of flowers in their yard. I remember the tiger lilies best, and their flower garden was edged with flat limestone rocks. At least once each summer, The Balloon Man gathered us kids around and he'd lift up one or two of those rocks. He then pointed out the fossilized remains of trilobites that were plainly visible and tell us about dinosaurs and other animals that lived long before we kids did.

One summer day The Balloon Man took us on a hike. The farms and fields around our neighborhood were just starting to become settled then and someone had punched a new road through a large woods some distance from our house. We explored that road, and The Balloon Man told us about different trees and bushes we saw that day. We ate crab apples and somehow, The Balloon Man was able to make a whistle out of a branch of a weeping willow tree.

The Balloon Man got his name because he was the only guy we knew who could "repair" balloons. Balloons were a rare commodity in those days. A kid who had a balloon was the envy of the neighborhood.

But if we had a balloon, invariably it would break. Off we would go to The Balloon Man's house with the pieces of colored rubber. "Can you fix this?" we'd ask him. "I think so" he'd say, "but I have to get my magic wand." The Balloon Man would then disappear into his house. Sometimes he'd be gone for quite a while. Then back he'd come with a funny hat on, and a straw, which he waved over the balloon. He'd put the pieces of our old balloon behind his back, and after a few *Abracadabras*, we'd be given our balloon back, all repaired. Sometimes The Balloon Man even *changed* the color!

I was almost a teenager before I realized The Balloon Man probably had been doing a switcheroo on us, telling us he was repairing our balloons when he was actually giving us new ones. Still, that hat and magic wand looked pretty authentic, and I guess if anyone could repair a balloon, The Balloon Man could.

Many decades later, I went back to the neighborhood for my father's funeral. I walked the alley behind The Balloon Man's house. The huge elm tree and the sandbox were gone. A garage had taken their place. But at Dad's funeral, an old man and woman came to pay their last respects. Despite the passage of forty years, I recognized The Balloon Man and his wife. They were now in their eighties, and though The Balloon Man didn't hear so well anymore, they still were sharp as tacks. I reminded them of their many kindnesses. The Balloon Man and his wife seemed surprised but pleased that I would remember.

The Balloon Man and his wife, through the little things they did, gave me wonderful memories that have lasted more than half a century and I remain grateful to this very day.

Chapter 6
Serving God

My folks were very strong Catholics and we kids were brought up the same way. They took us to Mass every Sunday, and once in a while, to early daily Mass. On Tuesday evenings Mom took us to Mother of Perpetual Help services. There was never any discussion about whether or not we should go to these services. We were expected to go, and that was that. So we went.

Like most Catholic families of those days, my folks always hoped and prayed that one of their sons would grow up to be a priest. They might have even settled for a daughter becoming a nun. Alas, it was not to be. Instead of becoming a priest, I became a lawyer. I hope Mom isn't too disappointed.

My godfather was my uncle Phillip Thullen. I have only a few memories of him. I clearly remember him building me a little wooden toy garage with a door that opened and shut. I really liked that garage[3] and played with it a lot. Uncle Phil and Aunt Bernice had no kids of their own and if my childhood early memories are accurate, Uncle Phil treated me like the son he never had.

On Valentine's Day, just before my fifth birthday, my Aunt Bernice walked to our house. She was crying, and it upset me because I had never seen an adult cry. Despite her tears, Aunt Bernice gave me a valentine card. It had a little boy holding a paper saw and the boy's arm pivoted so that the paper saw moved back and forth. Somehow I clearly remember

---

[3] Thinking back on it, I realize now that garage was probably made from the plans for a birdhouse, with Uncle Phil adding a little door so I could put toy cars in it.

what that card said … "I *saw* you Valentine!" Later I found out my uncle Phil had died that morning.

From an early age, we were taught each of us had a guardian angel who was assigned to us to keep us out of trouble and "on the straight and narrow." When I imagined how my guardian angel looked, I always pictured him looking like Uncle Phil Thullen.[4]

A kid's First Confession (now called the Sacrament of Reconciliation), First Communion, and Confirmation were always reasons to have family parties with lots of food. My relatives usually brought presents for the youngster who was undergoing those stages of growth in their Catholic religion, so there was some recompense for having to wear those white pants and white shirt and tie (for the boys), or a white lacy dress (for the girls). Things seem a lot less formal in the Catholic Church today.

The biggest trauma of my young life was trying to learn Latin so I could become an altar server. My folks probably figured getting their sons to serve Mass was a good start for the priesthood.

The nun in charge of altar boys was Sister Christella. She had us prospective altar servers meet once or twice a week to grill us on how we were coming in learning our responses to the priests who in those days said all Masses in Latin. If I recall, it took me a year or two to learn those responses well enough to pass Sister Christella's rigorous examination. I had nightmares for several years thereafter in which Sister Christella yelled at me for not remembering the correct Latin response.

All servers would get a monthly mimeographed Mass schedule and we were expected to be in church and suited up at least fifteen minutes before Mass started. Sometimes we served Mass on Sundays and other times we served Mass during the week.

As I related earlier, we lived on a tract of land that had once been the boyhood home of General Billy Mitchell. About four blocks away was the old Mitchell family mansion, which had been turned into an old folks'

---

[4] Several years after my Uncle Phil died, Aunt Bernice married Fred Heupler. Uncle Fred was a terrific uncle to have. In my younger years, Uncle Fred was a wholesaler of candy, delivering it to businesses around Milwaukee. Whenever I went to visit him, he'd take me out to his truck filled with candy and let me pick out what I wanted. About the time I reached my mid-teens. Uncle Fred got out of the candy business and began selling cigars. As before, when I visited he'd take me out to his truck filled with dozens of types of cigars and let me pick what I wanted. It is hard to imagine having a better uncle than that! Too bad he wasn't a banker!

home. Nowadays they call such places senior residences or assisted living centers, but to us it was just "the old folks' home." The Mitchell mansion was quite a place, built in the latter part of the nineteenth century. Every room in the home was decorated with materials from a different country. There was a room furnished in bamboo and another furnished in Italian marble. Two big painted concrete dogs guarded the front driveway, just as they had when the Mitchells were in residence[5].

Most servers didn't like to serve Mass at the old folks' home. It was a seven-block walk from Saint Rita's where we regularly served Mass, and in winter, those were long, cold blocks to walk. Furthermore, the old folks smelled funny and weren't always friendly to young kids, or so we thought at the time. My Dad had always said, "Be kind to old folks because, God willing, you'll be one someday," and I've always remembered and tried to practice that admonishment. Dad practiced what he preached. For several years he played Santa Claus at the old folks' home Christmas party and on at least one occasion, I got to dress up and act as Santa's helper.

I kinda liked to serve Mass at the old folks' home because of the nuns. The nuns who worked there had no kids of their own so they enjoyed fussing over those of us who came to serve Mass. Once Mass was over the nuns insisted we stay for breakfast and they'd set up a table for us in the kitchen, away from the old folks who smelled funny. We could order anything we wanted for breakfast and there would be bacon and eggs, pancakes, waffles, ham, sweet rolls, donuts, fresh bread, butter, and whatever else we could imagine. Even then I was somewhat of a trencherman and so I always enjoyed those breakfasts.

I do remember several embarrassing moments as an altar boy, one of which took place at the old folks' home.

It was Palm Sunday and the priest told me that before Mass began, I should pass out palms to everybody in church. "Don't try and carry too many palms at a time," the priest advised.

Palms can't be very heavy, I reasoned, and so I ignored Father's advice. I grabbed a big armful of palms and started down the aisle toward the front of the church. I was right-the palms weren't heavy. But Father was

---

[5] I found out later that General Billy Mitchell and I had a lot in common. We both went to Alaska, and we both loved Alaska. General Mitchell, as a lieutenant, was sent to Alaska, where he completed the telegraph line from Valdez to Eagle. Years later, General Mitchell stated to a Congressional Committee, "I believe that, in the future, whoever holds Alaska will hold the world ... I think it is the most strategic place in the world."

right too-I shouldn't have tried to carry too many. I quickly learned palms are slippery and no matter how tight I grasped the bundle of palms, more and more of them kept slipping out of the bundle. By the time I got to the front of the church, the aisle looked like a jungle floor. It was littered with palm fronds from one side to the other. Father, who was waiting at the back of church, was most unhappy. I was most embarrassed. And the old folks were quite amused.

On another occasion I was rushing down a dark hallway between the church and the chapel, carrying the collection basket full of money, when my sleeve caught on a door handle. My arm stopped but the collection basket did not. It flew some ten feet and then bounced down a flight of about a dozen stairs scattering money everywhere. It took me about an hour to pick up everything. When I got home I found $2.10 in change in the cuffs of my pants, so I had to walk all the way back to church to return it.

None of these things, good and bad, would have happened to me if I hadn't been an altar boy and I wouldn't have been an altar boy if it wasn't for Sister Christella. While I was in eighth grade, Sister Christella was transferred to another parish school. After all these years, I'm not sure why but a buddy and I rode our bikes that summer to the other school to see Sister Christella. We dutifully rang the doorbell to the church convent and Sister Christella herself came to the door. "What are you doing here?" she asked. Then she quickly told us we shouldn't be there and closed the door in our faces. That was the last time I ever saw her.

When I think back, I'm not sure Sister Christella had too many good days. She certainly would not have been in contention for any "Sister Congeniality" contest.

Chapter 7
Maybe This Is How I Got Started in Gun Collecting?

Carl Burbach was a friend of my father's and lived in Milwaukee in the later 1940s. He was a gun collector. We had an old sword in our basement with a straight, unsharpened blade, a black handle, and a bear's head on the pommel. I've never seen another like it. One day the sword was gone. My Dad said he gave it to Mr. Burbach "who collected that stuff."

I must have been five or six when I saw Mr. Burbach's gun collection. I don't remember much about it except he had a bunch of pistols and revolvers on a wall in a back room of his house. What I do remember, however, was Mr. Burbach gave me a cap pistol. That was more than sixty years ago and I still remember his kindness to a little kid.

That cap pistol may have gotten me started in gun collecting, because thereafter I was able to gather quite a few toy pistols. One had a long barrel and was made of tin. It went clickity-clack when the trigger was pulled. I have a picture of myself with that weapon wearing my cowboy hat (red with white lacing) perched on the top of my head, a vest, and a real neat pair of chaps.

In those golden days of yesteryear having the right cowboy clothes was just as important as having the right gun. Once every year or two a man would come around the neighborhood with a pony and a camera. He'd ring the doorbell and ask if any kids lived in the house. When he found a house that had kids, and most of them did, he'd offer to take the kid's picture astride the pony. I always wondered how that guy could make any money. He couldn't have charged too much, since I never heard of any kid in our neighborhood not getting his picture taken because a parent thought it cost too much. And I don't remember my folks complaining about the cost either. But certainly, whatever the man lost in the way of potential profit by keeping the price low, he didn't make up in volume either, because after our folks agreed that we could have our picture taken, he had to wait patiently outside while we got into our cowboy outfits.

After all, no self-respecting kid would be seen atop a horse or anywhere else for that matter, without his or her trusty six-shooter and Stetson. Five, ten, or even fifteen minutes later we'd be ready. There we'd sit, all decked out, high up on the pinto pony while the man took our picture. Many of the kids from my generation still have those pictures and treasure them. I know I do mine.

The author on a pinto pony in his front yard (circa 1948).

The kids in the neighborhood who weren't home when the man came around, often didn't believe a man with a pony had come into our neighborhood. In such cases, sometimes we'd be lucky enough to be able to show the doubting kid a place where that pony had "taken a dump" on our front lawn.

I still remember the best set of guns I ever owned. I got them for Christmas. They were called "49-ers." They were nickel-plated with some sort of "engraving" all over them. The grips were ivory-colored plastic and had a genuine red plastic ruby in each along with a raised carving of an ox team pulling a covered wagon. The cylinder actually rotated, and you slid the left grip aside to put in a roll of caps. I had a carved-leather belt and double holsters for the 49-ers as well as a matching set of what we called "cuffs". These cuffs snapped around your wrists like the tops of gloves and also were made of carved leather, with real plastic diamonds and rubies on them.

I came across a set of cuffs several years ago, and bought them, even though my wrists have grown too big to allow them to be snapped on. Sometime later I found a 49-er for sale. It cost me $125 but I didn't hesitate. I'd like to find another, as well as the holster set they originally came in. Now that I live in the Forty-ninth State, the significance of the "49-er" name is not lost on me.

Many of our guns, when we were kids, were cap guns. You can't find caps any more. Caps generally came in a box of 250 for a nickel. The good ones were made by Kilgore and had fifty shots to a roll. You'd buy a box, and then break the rolls apart as you needed them. Kilgore caps made a sharp bang when they went off, and there was plenty of smoke as well as the acrid smell of burnt gunpowder.

Nowadays there are many people who say kids shouldn't have toy guns at all. They claim that toy guns foster aggressive tendencies in kids. I never thought that aggressive tendencies were bad. I'd rather have aggressive, assertive kids than passive, apathetic kids.

Our kids all had toy guns when they were very young. Barbara and I let them have these guns, even though we had real guns in our home, because toy guns allowed me to teach our children proper gun safety at an early age. The kids learned that pointing a gun at a person, even if the gun was "only a toy one," resulted in harsh penalties which included "unilateral disarmament." They quickly learned to always watch where the muzzle was pointed, and such training served them in good stead when they started handling real guns later.

I've owned quite a few guns since my set of 49-ers. But I still like to pick up the little nickel-plated, engraved, ivory-handled, plastic-ruby-inlaid pistol with an ox team pulling a covered wagon. And I think of Carl Burbach and his kindness to me so long ago. Carl, wherever you are … Thanks for getting me started on a fascinating hobby!

The author with a cap pistol (circa 1948). The cap gun has just gone off and the smoke from the cap is drifting away over the author's right shoulder.

Chapter 8
The Little Bufalo

Growing up in a suburb of Milwaukee I didn't have much contact with firearms-no one in our family hunted and the only guns in my then limited arsenal were toys. I grew up during the final days of the "B Westerns" and after Dad bought our first TV set, we kids hurried home from school, strapped on our cap guns, and hunkered down to watch Hoppy, Roy, or Gene ride the range on the black and white screen.

When I was about seven or eight years old I came to the realization my father must be a criminal. Naturally, it was a very traumatic experience for me to come to that conclusion.

Of course, my friends knew my father must be a criminal long before I did, despite the fact that we all watched the same movies on the Westinghouse TV after school. Those movies clearly implicated my father beyond a reasonable doubt to every kid in the neighborhood but me. After all, in every Johnny Mack Brown and Randolph Scott movie, the villain invariably had a black mustache and was usually the only one to have such a mustache. Oh, there were other mustaches on some of the old-time cowboys, or on the hero's comical sidekick-like Gabby Hayes-but those were gray mustaches and they didn't count.

Things were a lot simpler then. We knew who the bad guy was when he first appeared in the film because bad guys always owned the saloon, always wore a black hat, and had a black mustache. In those days, no one asked-and we didn't care-if the villain had not been loved as a kid. He was simply "the bad guy" and we didn't question the reasons behind his behavior. We wondered, from time to time, of course, why the bad guy wasn't smart enough to shave his mustache off or wear a different-colored hat, so that it wouldn't be so obvious he was a crook. Mostly though, we just enjoyed the story without such in-depth analysis. Once a guy with a black moustache appeared on the screen, we kids knew that guy was the one who eventually would be exposed for his villainous deeds.

Unfortunately, my father had a black moustache.

My father had a black moustache.

Black moustaches weren't the only giveaway. The villain also always wore a black hat. It could be a big hat or it could be a small hat, but if it was black, without fail, by the end of the picture, the wearer would come to a bad end.

My father wore a black homburg.

The kids told me not to trust him, but I was loyal and defended Dad as long as I could. I defended Dad until I, too, became convinced he must have criminal tendencies. I became convinced when one day I happened to climb on a chair to look in Dad's top dresser drawer. Under some handkerchiefs I found a small black pistol, a Spanish .25 caliber Bufalo[6]. In my youthful ignorance I believed nobody had small black pistols except the police and criminals, and I knew my Dad wasn't a policeman. I also knew Dad had lived in Chicago during Prohibition while Al Capone lived there, and for a long time I wondered what Dad had done in Chicago before I was born.

The little Bufalo.

I learned later the pistol was acquired by my grandfather shortly after the First World War when he traveled throughout the United States for the Allis Chalmers Manufacturing Company repairing steam turbines. He met a Texan who had an old Colt that needed repair, and Grandda agreed

---

[6] No, I didn't spell Bufalo wrong. The Spanish did!

to take the Colt to Milwaukee and have it repaired. While the Colt was at the gun shop, the shop was burglarized and the Colt was one of the firearms stolen. Because of the war, firearms were in great demand and in short supply. The owner of the shop was able to get only a small supply of Spanish automatic pistols to replace the firearms that were stolen, and he gave one to my grandfather to replace the Colt. The Texan was a revolver man, however, and refused to take the little automatic. He told my grandfather to keep the pistol. I understand Grandfather carried the little pistol from time to time in his travels, especially when he went to Mexico during the early thirties, but he never shot it. He later gave it to my dad, who kept it in his dresser drawer, where I spotted it. Dad never shot the little automatic either, but gave it to me when I reached the age of eighteen.

I've now given the little pistol to my oldest son and told him the story of his "criminal black- mustached" grandfather.

Chapter 9
My Ugly Older Sister

There is a famous story called *The Ugly Duckling*. My sister Kay spent her teenage years as an ugly duckling. She wasn't ugly really-just plain as a post. Kay and my dad used to tell the story about her high school prom. When no one invited Kay to go to the prom, my dad secretly hired a guy to take her. Dad paid the guy fifty bucks, so the story went, and Dad even bought the flowers. The guy took my sister to the prom. Fifty bucks, in those days, was a lot of money. Later my sister found out Dad paid a guy to ask her to the prom and she was devastated.

Being the little brother, I thought my sister was beautiful. She was also very good to me. Kay, realizing that her little brother was a total nerd, did everything she could to make me cool. She'd buy me neat sweaters, and other trendy clothes. She'd give me encouragement and advice at every opportunity. She was everything a big sister should be and more.

I, of course, worshiped her.

In 1956, a local TV station held a beauty contest. The winner, to be named "Miss Channel 19," would win a red 1956 Buick Special convertible, a $1000 wardrobe, and a trip for two to Mexico. The first few runners-up would win a TV set. I wanted my sister to enter that contest. I told her if she didn't enter on her own, I'd pick out a picture of her and enter the contest for her. I figured we would at least win a TV!

Of course, the only pictures we had of Kay showed the ugly-duckling aspects. After I bugged her to enter the contest for several weeks, she went out, had her hair styled, and had a glamorous picture taken of herself which she submitted to the TV station. Lo and behold, Kay won the contest.

Even though I didn't get to go to Mexico, and got no part of the $1,000 wardrobe, when I got old enough to drive she'd let me take that Buick to school once in a while, or to take out a special date. It was a gorgeous car and really fun to drive.

My sister Kay and the 1956 Buick Special she won in the Channel 19 beauty contest.

A year or two later, having developed confidence in herself, my sister entered the Miss America contest. She was first named Miss West Allis, having won the local contest in our hometown, and then went on to win the Miss Wisconsin contest. Eventually my sister went to Atlantic City and was on TV in the Miss America Pageant with Anita Bryant in 1958. Kay and Anita were friends for a number of years.

My sister, like me, is now a senior citizen, and yet she is still gorgeous and often has guys in their thirties and forties ask her out. In fact, when anyone sees us together and learns that this lovely lady is my sister, invariably they ask me "What happened to you?" I just tell them I was adopted.

Chapter 10
Higher Education - High School

There was never any doubt in my mind that I would go to college. Marquette University was the big Jesuit Catholic University in Milwaukee and most local Catholic kids hoped to go there. To improve my chances at getting into Marquette, my folks wanted me to attend the university's prep school. Since Marquette University High School (MUHS) was a very prestigious school, I first had to pass an entrance exam.

I can remember taking the bus downtown one Saturday morning with two of my buddies to take this test. The test was a lot more difficult than the one I had taken to get into kindergarten. Nobody asked, for example, which bunny was different. Instead, there was a lot of English, Math, and reading comprehension. When it was over, my buddy Frank and I had passed. Our buddy Tom did not.

The fall of 1956 I started at MUHS. By this time we had moved from the little house on South 57th Street to a new house several blocks away at 5930 West Fillmore Drive. I lived at that address until I moved to Alaska.

My older sister, Kay, regularly drove me to school in her red Buick convertible. We'd often pick up Frank on the way. My sister worked downtown at Marquette University and when she went to work, she had to drive right past MUHS. So it made sense that we rode with Kay.

Unfortunately, Kay often didn't leave the house until 8:05 AM-and sometimes even as late as 8:20. MUHS started at 8:30 AM so it was usually a scramble to get to my high school on time. Kay had a regular route downtown, avoiding most stop lights and busy streets. She generally exceeded the speed limit. I loved the speed and excitement. Frank was often terrified. Like me, however, he did like the admiring glances of our classmates when we arrived at MUHS and got out of a big red Buick, driven by a pretty girl.

Despite my sister's giving Frank a ride to school most days, Frank never offered her any money for gas. The only time Frank gave my sister anything for her driving him to school was one Christmas when he gave her a tin of candy. She opened the tin, thinking perhaps that she had misjudged Frank. *Maybe Frank wasn't as tight with funds as he seemed to be?* Alas, just when we thought that maybe Frank had become generous, he announced that his mother had received the candy as a present at Christmas "but she doesn't like that kind, so I thought I'd give it to you. Merry Christmas!"

The way Frank held on to money, I figure by now he's a millionaire several times over!

MUHS was an boys-only high school, one of several Catholic all-boys high schools in Milwaukee in those days. In the fall, our school would play football against the other Catholic all-boys high schools. There were also several all-girls high schools. I didn't know much about girls. We never played football against the girls schools. Indeed, for the first few years of high school, I thought that girls were just boys who couldn't play football.

The all-girls schools would invite us to their dances, and we'd go happily. We'd invite the girls to dances at our school but only a few girls would show up. After a few MUHS "mixers" as we called them in those days, I stopped going. I wasn't very good at dancing, there weren't enough girls to go around, and I sure wasn't interested in dancing with guys.

Father Jerome Boyle, S.J., God rest his soul, was the vice principal at MUHS. Father Boyle carried a wooden golf club. The club's head had been cut off. I think it had once been a nine iron. The handle was made of hickory and whistled as it cut through the air. We whistled too when it hit us on the posterior. Father Boyle's command "Assume the position" generally meant we had somehow transgressed. When commanded to assume the position we placed our hands on our knees and bent over. Punishment varied from one to five swats. One was bad enough. Five swats at a time was reserved for only the very worst behaviors. If a student survived five swats, he was held in awe by fellow students for at least a day.

When MUHS grads get together, despite the passage now of some fifty years, the one teacher remembered above all others is Father Boyle. Though he was the most feared teacher in the whole school while we were students, he was the most revered once we were out. His title was Dean of Discipline and discipline was what he taught. We didn't learn it from books.

We learned it from his stick, and unlike many book subjects we have long since forgotten, we never forgot the lessons Father Boyle taught us.

It was hard to get into MUHS, since the school always had far more applicants than it had classroom space. The school had been around for more than one hundred years and it was not uncommon for three or four generations of one family to have attended the school. Discipline was one of the school's selling points. Our folks thought that if they sent us there, we would have less chance of getting involved in the type of shenanigans public-school kids got involved in. Father Boyle kept us on the straight and narrow. Our folks liked that at the time. We all appreciated it in later life.

If Father Boyle were alive and did today what he did then, he'd be in jail for assault.

Each year's class was divided into several sections. For example, the freshman class was divided into F-1, F-2, F-3, and so forth, all the way to F-7. The sophomore class was S-1, S-2, and so forth. The first two sections were the really smart guys. I started in F-4 and later was dropped to F-6. I stayed in the 6 section all the way through MUHS. Although we all had to study Latin the first two years, the really smart guys were taught Greek their last two years of high school. I don't remember what the 3s to 5s studied their last two years but we dummies in the 6s and 7s got to choose between Spanish, French, and German. I took German and, later in life, I was glad I did. But that is another story.

One class I remember in particular is Typing. Milwaukee was the city where the typewriter was invented around the time of the Civil War, and everybody at MUHS had to learn to type. If I recall, my teacher's name was Mr. Witas. He reminded me of Walter Mitty, a character from fiction who, at that time, was being played on television by an actor named Wally Cox. Mr. Witas looked just like Wally Cox, and acted like Walter Mitty, on Walter Mitty's off days. He was short, not very macho, and so the kids in my class could get away with anything in Typing 101.

In those days, nobody knew anything about word processors or computers. Indeed, in my school, nobody seemed to know much about typewriters. I still firmly believe that my school had purchased its typewriters from the original inventor, or perhaps from Civil War surplus because, even now, when I occasionally see an antique typewriter for sale, invariably it is a much newer model than the ones we learned on. In fact, once I graduated from my high school, I never again saw a typewriter like the ones we had in school.

The typewriters we used had little glass windows in their sides. We surmised that these windows were installed because typewriters were such a new invention when our typewriters were made, people wanted to see how they worked. To do that, all you had to do was press a key, while watching through the little windows, and you could observe everything moving inside. We used to look in the little windows often. It was much more interesting than listening to Mr. Witas.

Somehow though, we learned about margins, and about indenting the first sentence in a paragraph. To do this on our typewriters, we had to lift a little lid on the back of the typewriter where there was a bar with little teeth in it corresponding to the spaces on a single line of print. If we wanted to indent our letter five spaces, we counted out five notches in this bar, pulled out a removable key from somewhere else on the bar, and inserted the key in the fifth notch from the left. Then when we hit the lever that moved the carriage, usually the typewriter would indent five spaces.

That system worked pretty well. I say usually, because sometimes someone swiped a couple of these removable keys. That really made things interesting, because when that happened, the carriage wouldn't ring the bell when we got to the end of a line on our letter. If the bell did ring, you were supposed to hit the lever and change to the next line of your letter. If the bell did not ring, we who were watching our fingers instead of the line we were typing, would continue blissfully typing on the same line until we went off the paper. Even then we might not notice we had typed too far on that line until the carriage, with our sheet of paper on it, left the typewriter and fell on the floor. When that happened, everyone laughed-except Mr. Witas-and commenced to ring the bells on their type-writers until the class sounded like a collection of Good Humor ice cream peddlers on a hot day in July. Generally, it took Mr. Witas a full five or ten minutes to restore order, and the student whose typewriter carriage had fallen on the floor had to start all over again on his letter.

Even though I achieved a passing grade in Typing 101, I swore never to touch a typewriter again. Later, when I had my own law office and had to type my own letters and pleadings, I began to appreciate what Mr. Witas had tried to teach us.

Another teacher was Father Healy, who taught sociology. Father Healy was a devoted anticommunist and his classes were interesting. We learned how the Soviets took over eastern Europe. We also learned about the Communist party and how it was planning to take over the United

States. Father Healy promised every one of his students at least a B grade if they joined the John Birch Society. I sure could have used that B but I decided that sounded like cheating. Instead, rather than join the John Birch Society, I'd just work a bit harder. I never did join the John Birch Society. I never got my B grade, either. Like most of my grades, I got a "gentleman's C" for the course.

During or shortly after the Hungarian uprising of 1956, all Marquette High students were called into the auditorium for an assembly. The principal began addressing the student body when a great big guy in a raincoat came walking up the aisle, climbed up on stage, and took over the microphone, pushing the principal aside. "We are taking over this school!" the big guy in the raincoat announced. Then, amidst noisy but precision marching, a squad of soldiers marched up both aisles on either side of the hall, with rifles at "port arms." They then turned and faced the student body. Finally the curtain rose on the stage and there was a water-cooled machine gun, manned by about five soldiers. The machine gun was pointed out at the students. The guy in the raincoat then proceeded to tell us what we were going to do, what we could not do, what we were going to learn, and what we could no longer study. Threats were made of having students shot if they did not comply.

Father Healy had arranged that program to show us what it was like to live in a totalitarian society. It was a good thing we didn't have any girls in the classes-they might have fainted! Some guys figured it out and thought it was funny. Others figured it out and thought it was interesting. Some didn't figure it out and were just scared or angry. I think I was one of those who figured it out but I'm not sure. I do know my most vivid memory some fifty years later is of that machine gun!

––––––

I had my first date when I was a junior in high school. She was, at that time at least, a blond. She had a cute figure, big eyes, and was quite opinionated. I don't know why she went out with me. Perhaps she felt sorry for me. I certainly wasn't one of the "cool" guys.

At the time, I was smitten with her. Now, thinking back these many years, I believe I was as much impressed with her father as I was with her. Her dad, Leo, was a probate attorney and one of the first attorneys I had ever met. Leo reminded me of Spencer Tracy. Leo knew everybody and everybody seemed to know Leo. Leo tried to attend most of the funerals on Milwaukee's South Side and it was a wonderful thing to see him work the room. He always had a twinkle in his eye and a good word for everybody, even the corpse. Not only did Leo make a lot of friends by doing so, but more importantly, he picked up a lot of probate work besides. The more I got to know Leo, the more impressed with him I became. Eventually, because of Leo, I began to think about becoming a lawyer.

Leo's daughter went out with me only a few times, but Leo and I remained friends until the day he died.

———

Even though my sister, Kay, often drove me to high school, going home was another matter. I had to ride the city buses home and the ride took close to an hour. Then I'd go to my after-school job, which was delivering newspapers for the *Milwaukee Journal*. I earned eight to twelve dollars per week, working part-time every day. Sundays were especially tough because I'd have to get up at around five AM to get the Sunday morning paper delivered on time. I still have a note from my father that I found on the kitchen table early one cold Sunday morning. It said, "Wake me if it is below zero and I'll drive you to get the papers. Love, Dad." My folks were very good to me.

I don't remember getting spending money from my folks; instead, I was expected to earn it. Tuition at MUHS was $225 per year, and my folks had a tough enough time paying such a large expense to keep me in school. Any extra money I made was saved for college.

Later I got a job as a bagger/stocker for Kohl's Food Stores. Soon I was promoted to what they called the "Inside Man Outside" position. I'd stand outside the door of the store, greet people as they entered, and then help them put their groceries in their car after they left the store. One of my bosses was Herb Kohl, whose father owned the grocery chain. When I felt I deserved-or simply needed-a raise I'd speak to Herb. Usually Herb would talk to his dad-or somebody-and see to it my request was granted. At the time I write this, Herb Kohl is a U.S. senator from Wisconsin. On the few occasions I've visited Capitol Hill, all I've had to do is send my card in to Herb and he's come out of his office immediately to greet me. Although we probably disagree on most of the major political issues, we've stayed friends for many decades.

Eventually I graduated from MUHS. Now it was on to college.

Chapter 11
Higher Education - Undergraduate - UW-M

Since money was tight, I decided to go to the State university for my first few years of college.

A counselor at the University of Wisconsin-Milwaukee (UW-M) told me, "You are not college material. You should consider enrolling in a vocational school!" I told him I was not interested in vocational school and intended to go to college. "You'll have to pass the entrance exam," he warned.

I took the exam and must have done all right because I started college the fall of 1960. I enrolled in the pre-commerce program which would lead to a business degree. I also signed up for the Army ROTC program. I learned a lot of things in ROTC, including how to take an M-1 rifle apart and get it back together, military tactics, drill and ceremony, and how the US Army was organized. I learned marksmanship and gun safety. I thoroughly enjoyed the experience. The first commandment of the military at the time was "Always look after your men!" I have never forgotten that rule and have tried to practice it ever since.

UW-M was on Milwaukee's far north side and it was a long trip by bus. Eventually I was able to buy my first car. It was a turquoise blue Volvo 444 and it looked like a 1948 Ford. Four cylinders. Weber carburetors. Floor shift. It cost me $810. My father told me not to buy it.

"Don't buy a foreign car!" my father warned. "You'll never be able to get parts for it!" I should have listened to Dad because he was right. My Dad was always right! The car didn't have an emergency brake. "It needs a new emergency brake cable," the dealer explained. So for the next six months that I had the car, I had an emergency brake cable on "back order" with the local Volvo dealer. I never did get that cable.

I've never owned another foreign car; ever since, like my Dad, I always "buy American."

UW-M had two campuses. One was on the north side of Milwaukee and the other was downtown. I'd take a bus between campuses because I'd often had classes on both campuses the same day. I had a classmate named Dale who must have weighed five hundred pounds. Everyone would race to get on the bus before Dale because it was fun to feel the bus drop six inches when he clambered aboard. I wonder what ever happened to Dale?

I was in an English writing class one semester and had to do a research paper. I did it on John Phillips Sousa and the Ragtime Era. I thought it was a great paper. Unfortunately, my professor didn't think so. He gave me a C- and scribbled on my paper "Your writing is more appropriate for a Sunday Supplement than for a research paper!" His comments were accurate and prophetic because, a number of years later, I got to write a biweekly column (*From The Arena*) for the *Anchorage Times*, and later for the *Anchorage Chronicle*.

While attending UW-M, I continued to work twenty-five to thirty hours per week. I worked at Kohl's food store, and also at Sears in the shoe department. Working while going to college didn't help me get the best of grades. At the end of my second year, I would have to choose what specific type of degree I would seek in the last two years. I needed a 2.3 average to get into the School of Commerce for my business degree. I had a 2.1.

About this time, I had one of those experiences that changed my life. We had a manager named Bob at the Kohl's Foods store where I worked. He was a great guy and all the employees and customers really liked him. Unfortunately, rumor had it that there was some pilferage at the store by the night stockers and Bob had been unable to ascertain who the culprit was. One day "Big Frank" came into the store. Big Frank was a large swarthy man who was reportedly Mr. Kohl's "troubleshooter." Big Frank looked like a Mafia hitman and in a way he was. Big Frank walked up to Bob's office in the front of the store and in a loud voice told Bob he was fired and that Bob needed to get out of the store. Bob was humiliated, the customers were embarrassed for him, and I was quite angry too. I didn't believe Bob should have been fired, but of course, that was not my decision. The manner in which a loyal employee like Bob was fired, however, was totally outrageous. If Bob had to be terminated, he should have been taken aside and given his pink slip. Instead, Bob was publicly shamed, and there was simply no reason for that.

I vowed that I would do my best to never put myself in a position where someone could ever treat me that way. If at all possible, I determined to eventually become my own boss rather than work for others. In short, I decided to become a lawyer.

The next day I sat down and wrote my buddy, Herb Kohl, a letter of resignation. I told Herb that although I appreciated his friendship, I could no longer work for a company that treated its employees in such a shabby way.

I then began steps to transfer to Marquette University for my last two years of undergraduate work. Marquette had a law school and UW-M did not. With two years of Marquette under my belt it might be easier to get into its law school than if I tried to get in straight from UW-M. And besides, unlike UW-M, I didn't need a 2.3 grade point to get into Marquette's School of Business. My 2.1 grade point would do just fine.

Chapter 12
Higher Education - Undergraduate
- Marquette

Marquette University (MU) was a much bigger school than UW-M and I didn't know too many people there. But MU was closer to my home so the commute was not so bad. I enrolled in the college of Business Administration and opted for a degree in production and personnel management. (Nowadays it's called human relations.) I also continued to work twenty-five to thirty-five hours per week.

There were, of course, a lot more Catholic girls going to MU then at UW-M. The computer age was just beginning about the time. Some far-sighted person established a computer dating service at the university. I thought I'd try it. For ten bucks, you got a form to fill out and turn in. The service would then plug the information from your form into a computer and match you up with MU girls who appeared to be compatible with you. I waited about ten days for the results of my match-up. When the envelope arrived, I opened it with great anticipation. Instead of a list of compatibles I found my $10 returned to me with a note saying they could not find anyone to match me with! The computer service politely suggested I reapply in another six months or so when they "might have a bigger selection." Getting my money back from a computer dating service certainly didn't build up my confidence and self-esteem.

After a while, however, on my own, I finally did meet several young ladies who would go out with me more than once.

One, who later became a teacher, was so terrific and good to me that I seriously thought about the possibility of marriage. But rational analysis caused me to realize that while this girl could have been right, the timing was not. I still wanted to become a lawyer, and it would not have been fair for me to ask her to wait several years until I graduated from law school. It also would not have been possible for me to try and support a wife while going through law school. So we parted reluctantly, at least on my part, and likewise I like to think on hers. We've remained friends, however, and she eventually married a really nice guy. Many years later I had the pleasure of having her husband and son as my fishing guests in Alaska.

Later I began dating another girl after she broke up with a guy she had dated since they both were fifteen. This girl had a great sense of humor coupled with an infectious laugh, and I thoroughly enjoyed the time I spent with her. She too, in time, might have possibly turned out to be "the one" but for the fact that her old boyfriend returned to her life and she returned to his. She told me she still loved him and she eventually married him. We, too, are still friends and I got a chance to have two of her sons visit us in Alaska for several weeks one summer.

One girl even asked me to marry her! We had dated only a few times but she was a lot of fun to be with. She had several brothers and she liked the outdoors. One Sunday I asked her what she wanted to do and she said, "Let's go fishing!" So we did. Who couldn't like a girl like that? She was due to graduate from college the following spring and I think she was panicking that she hadn't found a husband. "Let's get married!" she said on about our fourth date. I was astonished. I told her that I was honored by the suggestion but that I wanted to go to law school and that we needed to get to know one another better before discussing marriage. "Take me home!" she ordered, and she never went out with me again. Three weeks later she was proudly displaying a diamond ring she had just gotten from an old boyfriend with whom she had rekindled romance. They were married within a year. Several years later I heard she and their unborn child were killed in a car crash.

I've been told that I met the woman who was later to become the love of my life during this time. Barbara Froelich was the president of a sorority at MU and I dated a number of girls from that sorority[7]. Barb says one or two of them introduced me to her at sorority functions but I sure don't remember that. Isn't it interesting that Barb remembered?

---

[7] I had to date a number of girls because most of them would not go out with me a second time.

During my undergraduate time at MU I pledged a fraternity, Alpha Delta Sigma, a professional advertising fraternity. My frat brothers and I had a lot of great times and great parties. Each year we picked a fraternity sweetheart. One year one of our fraternity sweethearts lived in a sorority house out on Highland Avenue. The fraternity brothers decided that we'd all go out there and serenade her. She had a room on the third floor of the house and she opened the window as we sang below. My fraternity "big brother" Bob "Animal" Jursch climbed two stories up the front of the building to seek a kiss. To get close to the window of our sweetheart's room, Bob had to inch out along the rain gutter some forty feet off the ground. Just after Bob got his kiss, the rain gutter let go. Thankfully, it did not break off the building all at once but instead broke off one nail at a time. Bob rode that rain gutter all the way to the ground, on two legs, never losing his balance. He hadn't earned the nickname "Animal" for nothing.

Those were interesting times, politically speaking. I can remember the Cuban Missile Crisis when it appeared the United States and the USSR might really engage in a nuclear war. None of us knew what to expect if "the balloon went up" and between classes we huddled in our cars, listening to the radio news. I do recall I carried a loaded pistol in the glove box of my car during that incident.

On 22 November 1963 President Kennedy was shot. All alive today who lived through that terrible event remember what they were doing when Lee Harvey Oswald shot John F. Kennedy. I was in a mathematics class when someone stuck his head in the doorway and shouted, "The President's been shot!" "Good!" responded my instructor. "Somebody should have shot that son-of-a-bitch long before this!" While other professors canceled classes so students could go to the Student Union and watch the developing story on TV, our professor continued to teach. As a result, it was a full hour after everybody else before we could find out the details of what had happened.

I thoroughly enjoyed MU despite its then "concrete campus" on the edge of downtown Milwaukee. I took business courses, including night courses on business law. The most enjoyable courses I took were speech and parliamentary procedure and I got As in both.

There were also mandatory philosophy courses such as ethics and logic. The one course that caused me the most problem was logic. I still have difficulty publicly admitting that I actually flunked logic!

In almost every other course, despite working long hours, I had to be content with a "gentleman's C." I needed a 2.0 grade point to graduate. My A grades in speech and parliamentary procedure gave me a total of four credits of As while my F grade in logic gave me a total of three credits of Fs. That extra credit of an A allowed me to graduate with a 2.09 cumulative grade point average.

I was the first person in my generation of our family to graduate from college. So what if, with a 2.09 grade point, my graduation was "by the skin of my teeth." I graduated and I had a bachelor of science degree in production and personnel management.

Chapter 13
The Home Front

While I was in college, I registered for the draft and received a student deferment. I never met anyone who had served in Vietnam until moving to Alaska in 1968. Although I had enjoyed ROTC, I wanted to be a lawyer rather than a soldier. I reasoned that if Uncle Sam needed me, he'd call, but so long as he didn't need me, I'd just keep working to become a lawyer.

I had a number of jobs during college. I sold shoes and worked at a grocery store. I even sorted bottles at the Grandpa Graf's Root Beer plant. In the summers, I worked for the West Allis Department of Forestry and Public Grounds cutting grass at the schools and parks, repairing cyclone fences, pulling weeds, and watering grass with a fire hose. During the summers I'd work fifty to sixty hours per week and during the school year I'd cut back to twenty-five to thirty-five hours per week.

I also was a "Momback." What's a momback? you might ask. A momback is the guy who works on the back of a garbage truck and signals the driver "C'mom back! C'mom back!" Working on a garbage truck all day when the temperature and humidity were both in the nineties was hard, smelly work. After two or three days in the sun, the garbage cans were full of maggots and I haven't worn cuffed pants or eaten white rice since.

Working for the city meant I was earning good money. I believe I started at $2.10 per hour and got all the way up to $2.65 per hour in the five or six summers I worked there. There were a lot of older fellows working on the same crew with me who were supporting their families on such wages.

———

With such good money, in addition to saving and paying for college, I was able to get rid of my foreign car, the 1958 Volvo, and get a good old American car. My dad and I went shopping together for a car to replace the Volvo. The first car we looked at was a used, bright red 1957 Chevrolet convertible. At the time it was selling for $1,095. (Now such a car would sell for more than $75,000!) Dad surprised me. Rather than rejecting such a sporty car immediately, Dad looked at the car long and hard and I think he would even have encouraged me to buy it. But then he noticed that someone must have left the convertible sitting out in the rain with the top down, because the rear floor was rusting out. Dad advised against buying the car and, unlike the Volvo purchase, I listened to him, although reluctantly.

Eventually I purchased a 1956 Chevrolet Bel Aire two-door hardtop. It was black with a white top and white trunk and stripe along the side. A real sharp car with a V-8 and a Powerglide transmission! I paid $625 for it. (Now it would be worth more than $50,000!)

I drove that '56 Chevy for several years until dad traded me his 1958 Chevy four-door sedan "even-steven." A year or two later I purchased a blue 1959 Buick LeSabre two-door hardtop. You don't see 1959 Buicks much anymore. It was long, low, and sleek, and had two big fins on the back, much like a rocket ship. Its trunk lid, with the fins, was almost as big as a dining room table.

The Buick was what we called, in those days, a "road car." That term referred to a big, heavy car, that held the road solidly at all speeds.

That Buick proved it was a road car on several occasions.

On one of our road trips, several of us guys drove from Milwaukee to Cleveland to visit an old friend, Tom Burrows. Tom had lived in Milwaukee, moved to California, and then to Ohio with his folks. We were good friends but seldom saw each other, hence our trip to Cleveland. We had a fun weekend there but wanted to leave Cleveland early Sunday morning, right after breakfast. We were staying at Tom's folks' house and his mother insisted we stay for a noon meal. She had cooked up a wonderful spread, as she always did, and we simply could not turn her down. As a result, we didn't leave her home and Cleveland until later in the afternoon.

Once it got dark, it started to get *really* dark. On the road back to Milwaukee, after a while we stopped seeing any lights except for our own headlights. We had taken the back roads home because we couldn't afford to pay the tolls on the Ohio Turnpike, but even so, it should not have been that dark!

I turned on the radio but couldn't find any AM or FM stations broadcasting. At the time, my radio also had a shortwave band and I finally found someone broadcasting via shortwave. Here's what we heard: "Attention! Attention! Persons in and around the vicinity of Fort Wayne, Indiana, are advised to take immediate precautions for their safety. A tornado has touched down in the vicinity of Fort Wayne and you must take cover immediately!"

Just as the warning came over the radio, we came around a curve only to see a sign reading "Fort Wayne-One Mile."

My old buddy, Thomas "Grandpa" Manning, was driving the Buick at the time and since I was more familiar with the car, we decided to switch drivers. Grandpa pulled over to the side of the road and slid across the seat while I opened the passenger door to go around to the driver's door. Once outside, I almost got blown off my feet. Outside the Buick the wind was blowing so strong I had to literally hold on to the car to get around to the other side. Inside the car, however, we could not even tell the wind was blowing.

The next hour or two we drove through scenes of utter devastation. Huge trees had been uprooted and lay strewn about. Homes were smashed. People were scurrying about with flashlights. More than 200 people were killed by a series of tornados that Palm Sunday weekend. Had we not stayed for Stella Burrow's wonderful dinner, we might have been in the middle of the worst of the storms. But the Buick plowed on through that night, as solid as a rock, carrying us all safely back home to Milwaukee.

My 1959 Buick was a real road car.

Over the Memorial Day Weekend in 1965 several friends and I were camping on an island at a place in northern Wisconsin called the Flambeau Flowage. On Memorial Day as we approached the boat landing, we saw a uniformed Wisconsin State Patrol officer standing on the dock. "Any of you guys named Ross?" he asked. After I identified myself, he informed me that my mother was dying and that, even if I hurried, I might not make it back to West Allis in time. "Your dad said to tell you that the choice is yours whether or not to hurry."

The author at the Flambeau Flowage in Northern Wisconsin (1965).

My mother had been ill with cancer for a long time. With her love of life, she would proclaim proudly that she had survived nine major surgeries in twelve years. I realized then that if Dad had involved the State Patrol, this time it was very serious.

Since our group of guys had several cars, I told the others to go back and take the camp down, and that I was going to try and make it back to Milwaukee in time to say goodbye to Mom. "I intend to drive hard and fast!" I stated, "and I don't care how many speeding tickets I get!" My high school buddy, Tom Zawodny, chose to go with me.

That big Buick had what we called a "ribbon speedometer." It unrolled from left to right. The faster you went, the more to the right the speedometer unrolled. At the far right of the dash, the speedometer pegged at 120 miles per hour.

Even though we were 310 miles from home, it was Memorial Day, we had to go through the outskirts of Madison, and we had to fill up the tank with gas, we covered the full 310 miles in three hours and forty-five minutes! That Buick just seemed to flatten out and hug the road. Most of the way the speedometer was pegged at the 120 miles-per-hour mark, as far to the right as it would go. We got sixteen miles per gallon for the trip! I never saw a cop and no cop ever saw me. I made it back in time to see Mom, who was dying of cancer, and we were able to say our final goodbyes. I will always be grateful to that old car for getting me there before she died.

As I said, that 1959 Buick was a real road car.

———

When I was in high school, I began to accumulate some firearms. I received no gun safety training from my folks. They weren't interested in guns, and they didn't know I was interested in guns either. In fact, my folks didn't even know I had guns because I sure didn't tell them!

I got no gun safety training from anybody else either. That led to a memorable misadventure.

The "Fat Plumber" was a neighborhood pal of mine named Greg. We called him the Fat Plumber because he was chubby, and because he wanted to follow in his father's footsteps and be a plumber.

The Fat Plumber and I were enjoying a quiet Sunday afternoon on the banks of the Fox River in southern Wisconsin. We had .22 caliber rifles with us. The Fat Plumber's dad knew he had a .22 caliber rifle but my dad didn't know about mine.

I had just shot at a target across the river when the Fat Plumber said something to me. I turned towards him to find out what he had said. As I did so, with the gun pointing towards the ground, I pumped another cartridge into the chamber. The gun, an old Model 1890 Winchester pump, went off. "Blam!"

When the rifle went "Blam!" I felt like an idiot. Just as I was going to apologize for scaring him, the Fat Plumber said, in a surprised voice, "Hey, you shot me!"

"Don't give me that!" I said. "I feel like a dummy already!" "No," Greg replied, "You did shoot me!" He then rolled up his pants leg and, sure enough, there was a neat hole through one side of his leg and out the other.

We got back to the car and I drove the Fat Plumber to the hospital where X-rays were taken. Thankfully, the bullet had hit nothing vital and three stitches on each side of his leg closed up the holes. After the Fat Plumber was given a tetanus shot, we drove home. When we pulled up in front of the Fat Plumber's house, his father came out on the front porch. "Gregory, you're limping!" his father said. "He shot me," the Fat Plumber said, pointing to me. "I shot him," I said, pointing to the Fat Plumber. "You guys and your guns!" said his dad, shaking his head, as he went back into the house. And that was the last thing that was ever said about the incident!

Nothing more, of course, needed to be said. The Fat Plumber's dad, God rest his soul, never squealed on me and as a result my dad, who was a friend of the Fat Plumber's father, never heard about the incident until I was about forty years old and chose to tell him.

Ever since that long-ago afternoon, I have been a strong advocate of proper firearms safety training.

———

My father was not a hunter; he was a fisherman. Although Dad did not get to fish as often as he wanted, when he went fishing, he usually took me along. One year, when I was about eight, Dad took me camping to Franklin Lake in the Nicolet National Forest in northern Wisconsin. We set up a tent camp. Dad had heard that a camper should always dig a trench around the tent so that if it rained, the water would not run into the tent. Dad dug a trench around the tent about six inches deep. Several campers came by and asked Dad if he was digging for gold, chiding him because his trench was so deep. That night it rained and almost everybody in the campground got flooded out. But Dad and I stayed nice and dry!

Dad rented a boat so he and I could go fishing. The boat-rental place was a mile and a half down the lake from our campsite. After a few quick lessons on how to row a boat-something I had never done-Dad pushed me off the shore and pointed in the direction of our camp. "I'll drive the car back to camp and you row the boat back. I'll be waiting on the shore at the campground."

For the first time in my life, I was in charge of my own watercraft. I was thrilled, although a bit apprehensive. Skirting the shore, I rowed and rowed and rowed. I finally saw Dad at the campground dock and took pleasure in having accomplished my first solo sea voyage.

Dad and I had a lot of fun together on that trip. We saw a number of bears and I even captured a chipmunk, which we took home to show Mom, later releasing it in the woods near our house.

That experience with Dad caused me to appreciate the outdoors.

———

As I grew older, my buddies and I tried to get out hunting and fishing as often as we could. When my folks learned I was interested in hunting, they supported me in that activity-probably because they knew I couldn't play basketball. We hunted squirrels or rabbits in the fall and winter at public hunting grounds outside Milwaukee or at various farms where we had permission to hunt. In those days, when we planned on going hunting during the week, we'd take our guns to school. Do that today and you'd get expelled and arrested!

We'd hunt deer in November, often along the Mississippi River near Durand in Pepin County. On one occasion the river bottoms where we hunted deer were crowded on opening day. That evening we went to the Thunderbird Bar where all the locals hung out and invariably, the talk turned to hunting. "J'get any?" someone would ask, and one of the guys in our group would respond as follows: "Nope … didn't see a deer! But I did get three or four 'sound shots.'"

"Sound shots?" the local would ask. "What are sound shots?"

We'd then explain that although we didn't actually see the deer, we'd heard something in the bushes and took a shot at the sound. The local would then ask in detail where we'd be hunting the next day. Of course, our story about sound shots wasn't true but the locals didn't know that.

All they knew was that a bunch of crazies were going to be hunting the next day, and those crazies were shooting at sounds in the woods. As a result, most of the time we'd have the entire swamp to ourselves the next day, the locals choosing to hunt elsewhere.

Sometimes we'd camp at Wyleusing State Park on the western border of Wisconsin. We would set up camp high on a bluff overlooking the Mississippi River and spend the days fishing or shooting at snapping turtles in the sloughs below the bluff. On one occasion an entire troop of cub scouts took over the campground, and our enjoyment of the area's serenity was thoroughly destroyed.

That evening, the scout troop built a big bonfire several hundred yards from our camp and all the scouts and their leaders gathered around singing songs, telling stories, and doing everything else that scouts do in such circumstances. One of my buddies, John Mietus, was very adroit at imitating the call of a wolf. John blackened his face, put on his darkest clothes, and snuck out into the night. Shortly thereafter, the howling of a wolf was heard, sometimes on one side of the scouts' campfire, and sometimes on the other. It really sounded like the troop was encircled by a large pack of wolves.

Soon flashlights were being trained on the woods and I heard one scoutmaster say to another "This is ridiculous! There are no wolves around here!" To which the other replied, "OK, smart guy … Then what is that noise?" The scouts didn't sleep much that night and at dawn they all broke camp and headed for home. Once again our serenity returned.

John tried out his wolf call for the last time in northern Wisconsin several years later. As we hiked back to our camp at Spyder Lake early one evening, John let out a wolf howl. In an instant, a large black timber wolf jumped right out of the brush into the trail directly in front of John. Which one of them was more surprised is debated to this day. I do know that John took off one way down the trail and the wolf took off the other way, leaving the rest of us laughing too hard to go either way.

———

Each year Wisconsin seemed more crowded and it became more and more difficult to get out in the wilderness away from others. Often, especially on major holidays such as Memorial Day, the Fourth of July, and Labor Day, we had to drive for hours to simply find a place to camp where we could imagine we were in wilderness. On one occasion, we took a dirt trail a mile into the woods and camped alongside the Wisconsin River north of Eagle River. That night some of the local high school seniors moved in across the dirt road from our camp, held a wild beer party all night, and somehow managed to steal all the food from our coolers, which we had foolishly left outside our tent.

As a result we began to take our adventures farther and farther afield. Twice we drove all the way from Milwaukee to the Canoe Trails of Northern Minnesota. Both were great trips but to get into real wilderness required taking a substantial amount of time off work and such trips we guys could afford only once or maybe twice a year.

———

I graduated from Marquette's College of Business Administration in December 1964 and applied for law school. With a 2.09 overall grade point in my undergraduate studies, I suppose I was unrealistic in the idea that I could get in to law school. But the thought never crossed my mind that I would be turned down. So I took the Law School Aptitude Test (LSAT) and did well. In fact, I was later told that I got the same score as the fellow who would graduate at the head of our class, although I don't know to this day if I really did that well. What I did know was that I got accepted for law school at Marquette University and that Mom was able to live long enough to know it too.

From December 1964 until September 1965, when my first law classes began, I went to work as a wholesale salesman for M. Weingrod and Associates, a wholesale distributor. I sold radios, tape recorders, and portable record players. I traveled all over the Milwaukee area visiting retail stores, attempting to sell Aiwa and Panasonic products. I liked the people I worked for, but I hated the job. At that time at least, salesmen were one step below rubbish collectors, or so it seemed to me. Often I drove across town to meet a store owner only to get the brush-off or I'd have to wait an hour or more before the store owner finally took the time to see me. I vowed then that I would always try to treat salesmen with proper courtesy thereafter, but never to become one myself.

Chapter 14
Law School

As we sat in the reading room of Marquette University's Law School that first morning, the law school faculty did its best to impress upon us the seriousness of the educational journey upon which we were about to embark. "Take a look to your right and to your left," Professor O'Connell intoned ominously. "At the end of three years, one of you won't be here!"

Professor O'Connell was correct in a way. At the end of the year, he was gone from the faculty and most of us never knew why. All we knew was that the good professor had alienated some of the curmudgeons who controlled the law school and he was "let go."

I don't know if the guy to my right and the guy to my left made it through three years but I was determined to do so. Law school was interesting, tough, boring, exciting, and terrifying, all rolled up into one experience.

We learned a lot about the law ... but very little about being a lawyer.

We learned how to research the law, but nothing about dealing with clients, earning fees, and running a law office.

Our education was classical but definitely not practical.

———

I have had some sort of job since I was twelve years old. My education was expensive and I always had to work to pay for it. Law school was no exception and while most law students could concentrate their full time on law studies, I could not. To afford to stay in law school I had to also have gainful employment. As a result I worked twenty-five to thirty hours a week in addition to attending school.

One of the best jobs I had during law school was working for the US Post Office. Every day after classes were out I'd go down to the post office garage, sign out a post office truck, and drive around town on a particular route picking up mail from the mailboxes. I had to keep a schedule because a mailman could not collect mail from a mailbox before the time shown on the outside of the box. I also stopped in at postal stations and picked up any registered mail the stations might have. I'd then take the registered mail back downtown to the main post office. I'd work from around 3:30 in the afternoon until nine or ten at night on weekdays and often four to five hours on Saturday or Sunday. I was outside most of the time, meeting people, and earning pretty good money. Before I left that job, when I graduated from law school, I was up to about $3.85 an hour.

If I was not working for the post office, I was selling shoes for Sears, Roebuck & Company at a store on Mitchell Street (or as the old-time Milwaukeeans would say "Down by Mitchell Street, where the streetcar bends the corner around"). I was guaranteed $2.10 per hour or a 10 percent commission, whichever was more. Generally I made more than my guaranteed hourly rate. I still say that job helped me to "face de feet (defeat)" well.

––––––

There were some interesting people teaching at Marquette Law. One was Judge Francis X. Swietlik. Rumor had it that Judge Swietlik once had Clarence Darrow as a student when Darrow was a very young man. Nobody knew when, or even if, Judge Swietlik had ever been a young man himself. In his eighties at the time I was there, Judge Swietlik had started teaching at MU long before World War II and in the many years he had taught, it appeared that the judge had never updated his lectures. "Here's a recent case from the Wisconsin Supreme Court," he'd begin. "It seems that the plaintiff was riding in a horse-drawn ice wagon when the wagon was hit by a streetcar … " Judge Swietlik was much beloved and an interesting character.

Another character was Professor Leo Leary, who taught tax and trusts and estates. "Here's a dime," Leo'd say to a student who failed to properly respond to a question. "Go call your folks and tell them you have decided to become a plumber!"

I remember being puzzled initially by one set of instructions Leo gave to our class regarding a forthcoming term paper. Leo announced that while he would not take off any points if the term paper was handwritten, he would give extra points if the term paper was typed. After

I thought about that statement for a little bit, the semantics were not lost on me. As a result, I had my cousin Rosemary, who was a paralegal, type my term paper. I have no doubt that John Houseman's character, Professor Kingsfield in the movie *The Paper Chase*, was derived from Leo Leary.

One of my favorite professors was James Ghiardi. Professor Ghiardi taught torts. He was a bright, enthusiastic teacher. He was always talking about "The Reasonable Man" and after presenting a fact situation, professor Ghiardi would always ask the question "What would the Reasonable Man do under such circumstances?" He seemed to ask me that question far more than the other students so that they began calling me The Reasonable Man. Every year I was chosen to play professor Ghiardi in the skit the students put on at the law school's annual Christmas party.

Professor Ghiardi had a lovely daughter named Jeannie. He kept Jeannie well hidden. No one knew professor Ghiardi had a lovely daughter until one of my buddies, Jim Duffy, somehow discovered Jeannie and started to date her. Duffy ended up with the highest grade anyone had ever gotten in professor Ghiardi's class. Later Duffy married our torts professor's daughter, moved to Hawaii, and eventually became a justice on the Hawaii Supreme Court.

———

I, too, met the love of my life while in law school.

In early 1966 my buddy John Mietus got married in Munster, Indiana. At a post-reception party, a friend from law school, R.E.B., and I were playing "life of the party," telling jokes and stories. That's when I met Barbara Froelich.

I was attracted first by her hairstyle and clothes. She was wearing a very sharp looking suit and I thought, "There is a well-dressed girl." Barbara was classy and really nice looking. She also seemed to have a great sense of humor because she was laughing at the jokes R.E.B. and I told. I remember thinking, "This is the type of girl I could marry," and then being surprised, and even a little worried, by such a thought.

R.E.B. beat me to the punch and asked Barbara out. Since he had done so and since he was a buddy, I didn't want to interfere by asking her out myself. Nonetheless, I wrote Barbara a letter. It was a really stupid letter, filled with puns and other nonsense. I got no response. I found out later that after she read the letter, Barbara was convinced I was a nutcase.

Several weeks later I asked R.E.B. if he was still dating "that Barbara what's-her-name."

Barbara Froelich, later to become Barbara Ross.

"Not me!" said R.E.B. "I couldn't get to first base with her. She's the type of girl you'd want to marry!"

Months passed but I couldn't get Barbara out of my mind. I asked John Mietus' wife about Barbara and she told me Barbara was now living in Milwaukee. I wanted to call Barbara and ask her out but I had heard she had reacted badly to my letter and had been convinced of my nutcase status. I finally came up with an idea. I told John I was going to have a New Year's Eve party and we should invite all our mutual friends and I specifically mentioned inviting everybody who had been at the wedding's post-reception party. I figured John and his wife would invite Barbara. John mentioned that maybe he'd invite Barbara. I, of course, said "Say, that's a good idea, John! I'm glad you thought of her!"

Later John told me he had invited Barbara and she said she'd stop at the party later on New Year's Eve. As a result of that promise, I didn't take anyone else to the party, using the excuse that I would have no time for a date because I'd be running the event. I figured I'd try and hustle Barbara if she came. But Barbara never showed up and I had a very disappointing New Year's Eve.

In early 1967, I went to the baptism of John and Phyllis Mietus's first son. They had mentioned to me that "the Barbara you met at the wedding in Indiana will be there." Since the baptism was on a Sunday afternoon and I was scheduled to work for the Post Office, I got somebody to work for me and went to the baptism. Barbara finally showed up late in the afternoon and we chatted briefly. Then I had to leave because I had a date that night with Christine K.

I hadn't taken Christine K. out before, but my older sister had loaned me her new 1964 red Buick convertible for my date that night and I figured with the convertible, I'd make a good impression on Christine. When I went to Christine's house to pick her up, however, she wasn't at home. She'd had an argument with her parents and left the house. I located Christine down the street but it was quite apparent she wasn't in the mood that night to go out on the town.

So here I was, like an atheist corpse in a coffin "All dressed up and no place to go!" I had on my best suit and I had a cool car, but no date for the evening. I decided to try calling Barbara. My buddy John had given me her phone number.

When Barbara answered the phone, I told her a friend of mine was playing the trumpet at a local nightclub and that I was going down there to listen. I asked her if she'd like to go along.

"Do you know what time it is?" Barbara asked.

"Sure," I responded. "It's 9 PM."

"I've already put my hair up," Barbara protested.

"That's OK," I said. "I'll give you an hour to get it back down."

Finally, Barbara agreed to my picking her up at 10:15 PM. And thus began a romance and adventure that has lasted more than forty years.

At the nightclub I told Barbara I was thinking about moving to Alaska. When she heard that, her old thoughts about my being a nutcase were resurrected. We had a nice evening and when I took Barbara home, I asked her for a date the following week. Unlike most girls, she agreed to go out with me a second time. As she has told others since, she wasn't dating anybody at the time and she "figured going out with this crazy guy who claimed he was going to move to Alaska was still better than sitting at home alone!"

After several dates, I realized that I could easily fall in love with this lady. So we had a nice long chat one evening and we agreed that we were both interested in dating further and in discovering what might develop between us.

———

The really smart guys were chosen for the *Law Review*. The *Marquette Law Review* was a collection of learned law articles published, every so often, in a soft-covered book. The articles were written by the really smart guys on some legal topic or another chosen by the faculty. If a student wasn't in the top 10 percent of the class, he didn't get asked to join the law review staff. Being on the law review staff was a great honor and looked good on a resume.

I didn't get asked to join the law review staff because I wasn't in the top 10 percent of my class.

In fact I wasn't even in the top 50 percent of my class. I think that one time I calculated that I was the top man of the bottom third of my class. Even if somehow I had been asked to join the law review staff, I really would not have had the time for it. Instead, in order to stay in law school, as stated, I had to work around twenty-five to thirty hours a week just to earn enough for tuition and books.

Besides the *Law Review*, there was another extracurricular activity at the law school that was somewhat prestigious. That was the Moot Court Team. The Moot Court Team took a hypothetical case, worked on it for several months, and then argued one side or the other before a federal district court judge. The really smart guys who didn't get on the *Law Review* would generally get on the Moot Court Team. As the top man of the bottom third of my class I had little or no chance of getting selected for either the *Law Review* or the Moot Court Team.

Professor Wally McBain was in charge of the Moot Court Team. Wally McBain did not look like a law professor. I always thought he looked like a high school girls' basketball coach. In the "real" world of the law school McBain taught real property.

One day McBain was lecturing on the topic of "lateral support." He pointed to the twelve-story girls' dormitory across the street and posed the hypothetical question, "If you were going to build another twelve-story building next to that dorm, and you had to first dig an excavation for the footings for your new building, how would you ensure the girls' dorm would remain standing until you could ensure the dorm had lateral support from your excavation?" He called on me for the answer. I had no idea how to ensure lateral support and told him so. It sounded more like an engineering question than a legal one.

"C'mon!" McBain chided me. "Surely you can think of something you could do to ensure lateral support during construction?"

My response that I would " … move all the fat girls to the far side of the dormitory?" did not endear myself to old Wally, although it did get some laughs.

Picture of a building that lost lateral support.

As I wrote earlier, the really smart guys who didn't get on the *Law Review* would generally get on the Moot Court Team. As a "C" student, I didn't have much expectation of getting either on *Law Review* or Moot Court.

But early in my junior year, a notice was put on the bulletin board inviting anyone who was interested in being on the Moot Court Team to submit an application to Professor McBain. I told McBain I intended to submit my application. "Go ahead!" McBain told me. "I'll be happy to reject you!"

Since I always enjoyed a challenge, I submitted my application. Maybe it was because McBain was in charge of the Moot Court program, or maybe God felt sorry for me. Whatever the reason, there were far fewer applications for Moot Court than ever before. Wally needed ten or twelve students. I was one of only seven who applied.

Instead of rejecting my application, Wally needed me!

In fact, he needed more than just me! He had to whine and cajole but he was finally able to round up five more and Wally had his Moot Court Team.

It took a lot of extra work to get ready to present our argument in the Moot Court competition. I can remember spending long hours in the law library, sometimes late at night. And yet it was a lot of fun. Finally we were going to get to act as lawyers.

The case we were assigned to argue was based on *Griswold v. Connecticut*, 381 U.S. 479 (1965). *Griswold* was a landmark case in which the US Supreme Court ruled that the Constitution protected a right to privacy. The Supreme Court found that a Connecticut law which prohibited the use of contraceptives was unconstitutional because it violated "the right to marital privacy."

On the night of the Moot Court Team Competition, the team members and their families all gathered in one of the large courtrooms of Milwaukee's federal courthouse. Federal district court Judge John Reynolds presided. Each of the team members got to make part of the argument. I was doing pretty well but Judge Reynolds interrupted to ask a question, as he did with everyone. The judge asked these questions, we were told, to ascertain how well a student knew the case. We were of the opinion, however, that the judge asked his questions to see if the person arguing would lose his or her train of thought.

Discussing privacy, the judge asked me, "Surely, Mr. Ross, there has to be some place where I can crawl and hide, safe from the prying eyes of the government?"

I responded by saying "Judge ... according to the finding of marital privacy in the *Griswold* decision, you can crawl into and hide in your bedroom, any time you want!"

The judge smiled. The gallery chuckled. Wally cringed. Wally was the only one there without a sense of humor.

Wally McBain got me back, a bit later, for my levity. Each member of our Moot Court Team had kicked in a couple of bucks so we could each have a plaque attesting to our being on the team. I was in charge of buying the plaques. I ordered a neat wooden plaque for each team member with "Moot Court Team" and his name on a brass plate. The plaque also had a small golden gavel.

In the spring of each year, the law school had an awards banquet. Usually every student went because it was one of the big events of the year. Being top man of the bottom third of my class I, of course, had never gotten an award at any of these functions but I always went to clap for those who did. This year, however, I knew I would get an award, one of the plaques, because I had ordered them myself. Tickets were very expensive but I made sure long in advance to invite Barbara. I told her that for the one and only time in my law school career, I was going to get an award and I wanted her to be there with me.

A lot of awards were given out that night. When it came time to present the awards to the Moot Court Team, each member was called to come up to the podium, one at a time, to receive a plaque. My name, however, didn't get called. I didn't get to go up to the podium and I didn't get my plaque … even though I had bought the damn thing myself!

"I thought you were going to get an award?" Barbara asked.

"So did I!" I replied.

During an intermission I approached Professor McBain and asked him why my name had not been read, and why I had not gotten my plaque. "Oh … " said Wally, "I must have forgotten. Well … you can pick up your plaque on Monday at my office."

So I did.

And it was the only award I ever got in law school. So what if I had picked it out and paid for it myself!

Chapter 15
Alaska Dreaming

During the late 1950s and early 1960s a few fellas from the neighborhood traveled all the way to Alaska. All of these were older guys who went to Alaska for some hunting or fishing. Invariably, upon their return, they'd rent the back room of some corner tavern, invite the neighborhood, and have a salmon or moose dinner. They'd show pictures from Alaska, either color slides or shaky 8mm movies. Most outdoorsmen in the area would attend. My buddies and I went for the beer, for a chance to taste the strange (to us) food, and for a chance to see Alaska. We all agreed that Alaska must really be a beautiful place and promised ourselves that some day, before we died, we'd visit Alaska for a few weeks of hunting and fishing.

Eventually I started reading about Alaska. The first book I read was James Oliver Curwood's *The Alaskan*. Another book I found fascinating was *Homesteading in Alaska*. Again I vowed that some day I'd take a two- to three-week vacation there and see it for myself.

Up until I was in law school, I hadn't really given any thought at all to actually moving to Alaska. My dad was an alderman in our hometown of West Allis and he and I both assumed that some day, maybe, I'd run for that job. Of course I'd wait until Dad chose not to run but the alderman's job would be a nice way of serving the community as well as possibly picking up some clients when I began my law practice.

But then one day in law school the professor mentioned a case "decided by the Supreme Court of Alaska." With a mind like a steel trap I realized that "if there is a Supreme Court in Alaska, there must be attorneys there!" Just that quick I decided to look into the possibility of moving to Alaska and practicing law.

At the law library I read what I could find about the legal profession in Alaska.

I checked with the alumni office and learned that there was only one Marquette Law School graduate in Alaska ... Michael Edward Monagle, MU class of 1929.

Michael Monagle lived and practiced in Juneau. If Monagle had lived in Juneau while attending Marquette Law School, traveling to school and back home must have been quite a chore. The late 1920s was before the establishment of regular air service to Alaska. To get to Marquette, Monagle would have had to take a ship from Juneau to Seattle and then travel by train from Seattle to Milwaukee. If he actually lived in Juneau while going to MU, I'm sure he didn't go back home over the Christmas holidays. It probably took him a week of travel each way between the university and home.

I copied the pages from *Martindale-Hubble*'s law directory that listed Alaskan lawyers and law firms. In early 1967 I wrote about forty letters to firms across Alaska looking for a summer job. Barbara was kind enough to type those letters for me. Most of my letters went unanswered. Michael Edward Monagle wrote that he was hiring his son as a law clerk for the summer and could not hire me but he wished me good luck. A guy named Stump in Ketchikan copied my letter and sent me the copy back on which he had tersely written "There is no place for you in Ketchikan! Suggest you try Anchorage, Fairbanks, or Juneau!" Several letters had nice notes but those lawyers who bothered to respond at all said, basically, that they were not interested in 'hiring a pig in a poke." They wrote that if I was really interested in coming to Alaska, I should come see them when I was "on the ground." As one fellow put it, "If you are in the neighborhood, stop in and see me."

Since I was paying my own way through law school (there were no student loans in those days except from Dad) I gave up the idea of a summer job in Alaska. There was just no way I could afford to take such a lengthy and expensive trip without having a job waiting for me in Alaska when I got there.

Chapter 16
My First Trip North

On Wednesday, during final exams of my junior year of law school, a fellow student approached me and introduced himself. "You don't know me," he stated. "My name is Jerry Shimek and I heard you talking about going to Alaska some day. I usually go somewhere each summer to work and after hearing you talk about Alaska, I decided to go there. I'm leaving Monday. Want to come along?"

I asked Jerry how he was getting to Alaska.

He told me that he had a 1961 Volkswagen Beetle and he was planning on driving the Alcan Highway. "You can help pay for gas and we'll split any other expenses!"

"What will we do there?" I asked.

"We'll look for jobs, stay the summer, and then drive back," he responded. "If we don't find any jobs we'll turn around and come home!"

I was taken aback. After receiving no promising leads from the series of letters I had sent earlier in the year inquiring about jobs as a law clerk, I had decided that Alaska was out for that year and I'd once again have to find summer work in Milwaukee. Now here was an offer worth considering. We talked a bit further and when I went home, I discussed with my dad going to Alaska. Although Dad didn't like to see me leave home, he agreed that I should "try it" and offered to loan me some money for expenses. I called Jerry back at home, told him to count me in, and we finalized plans.

I still had my job at the post office and it was a good one. I wanted to be able to go back to it in the fall when I returned to law school. So I made an appointment to see the Milwaukee postmaster, Cy Cybulski. Mr.

Cybulski had a big office in the downtown post office and he greeted me amicably. When I told him that I wanted to go to Alaska for the summer and hoped that I could return to work at the post office in the fall, Mr. Cybulski promised to have my job waiting for me when I got back. "I always wanted to go to Alaska!" he stated. "I wish I could go with you!"

Early on the morning of 5 June 1967 Jerry pulled into my driveway to pick me up. While we were loading the Volkswagen, Barbara came by to see us off. She had packed us a large lunch of turkey sandwiches. I again realized that here was a special girl. She had driven all the way from downtown just to say goodbye! I wondered whether I was being foolish in leaving this girl behind to seek adventure in Alaska. However, I shook my dad's hand, gave Barbara a kiss, and off we drove, headed northwest.

That night Jerry and I camped in a highway wayside in North Dakota near Fargo, spreading our sleeping bags out under a starry sky on a couple of vacant picnic tables.

The author in the Dakotas on the way to Alaska for the first time (1967).

The next day we continued northwest towards Saskatchewan. I had been told that Canadians didn't like handguns and required all travelers to Alaska through Canada to declare such firearms to Canadian Customs. The handguns would then be placed in a sealed plastic bag which had to remain sealed while the traveler was in Canada. It could only be opened without penalty upon leaving Canada. I had brought two handguns along on the trip, a Smith &Wesson K-22 .22 caliber revolver and a Smith & Wesson 1950 Target revolver in .45 Colt. When we attempted to cross the border into Saskatchewan at North Portal, North Dakota, I dutifully declared my revolvers.

"You can't bring those handguns into Canada!" the border guard announced. When I questioned him, however, he admitted that taking sealed hand guns through Canada was allowed in the provinces of Alberta and British Columbia. They just weren't allowed at all in Saskatchewan. At his suggestion, we drove a few miles back into North Dakota and stopped at a Railway Express Agency. It cost only a few bucks to ship my two revolvers to myself in Anchorage. They were marked "Hold for arrival." Now I had to get to Alaska, if only to pick up my guns!

In those days, however, it was OK to bring long-guns into Saskatchewan. I had a short-barreled twelve gauge single-shot shotgun. I guess it could have been called a short-barreled long-gun and I kept it with us in a case behind the VW's front seats. We were going to be going through some rough country and my mom, Mrs. Ross, hadn't raised a dummy. I don't make it a practice to travel off the beaten path without having some kind of firearm handy, and I didn't then either.

After shipping my revolvers we drove back to the border crossing at North Portal. I showed the Canadian border guard my shipping receipt and we were welcomed into Canada.

The Province of Saskatchewan was somewhat of a disappointment. I had seen the old Alan Ladd movie *Saskatchewan* wherein Ladd fights the mighty Sioux amid forests of magnificent trees. There aren't any magnificent trees in the real Saskatchewan. In fact, there are hardly any trees at all!

Saskatchewan is flat as a pancake. Without any real trees, the highest objects we saw were grain elevators. We could almost have tied the wheel down and slept all the way across Saskatchewan. It was like driving across a pool table. We slept that night at a campground outside Davidson, Saskatchewan.

The only thing in Saskatchewan that wasn't boring were the names of the towns. Moose Jaw. Saskatoon. Battleford. Lloydminster. Unfortunately, the names of the towns were a lot more colorful than the towns themselves.

Then we entered the province of Alberta. We went through Edmonton and then through Valley View. There wasn't much of a view of any valleys, however, because of the smoke from a large number of forest fires in the area.

We rented a motel room in a town called Grande Prairie. After camping in a tent for several nights, it was good to get a shower! I still remember the setting sun shining golden on the prairie grass surrounding that town.

The saloons there had a separate entrance for women. I have no idea why there were separate entrances for women especially when we didn't see many women in any Canadian bars. Maybe Canadian women didn't come to the bars because they didn't like to have to open their own doors? Who knows?

The next morning we drove to Dawson Creek, British Columbia, the start of the Alaska-Canada (Alcan) Highway. We stopped at the Alaska Café for breakfast and had our pictures taken at Milepost 0, almost a mandatory tradition in those earlier days of driving the Highway.

After leaving Dawson Creek, we had eighty-four miles of pavement before beginning to drive the 1,200 miles of gravel that constituted the real Alcan Highway. Once the pavement ended and the gravel started, it began to rain. The VW was running fine, even though the highway turned to gumbo.

We stayed overnight in a motel at Fort Nelson, British Columbia, Milepost 300. Less than 1,000 more miles of gravel to go!

About 9 AM the next day, after filling up with gas, we again hit the road heading for Whitehorse, Yukon Territory. Gasoline was 55.9 cents for a gallon of regular and we paid as high as 60.9 cents per gallon on the Alcan Highway. But the gallon in Canada is called the "imperial gallon," which is one fifth larger than an American gallon.

I had sent Barbara a postcard from Dawson Creek with the note, "We've put on almost 2,000 miles so far and the car is running good." My comment must have jinxed everything because ten miles out of Fort Nelson, the VW's engine started sounding funny. We turned around and limped back to Fort Nelson to have the engine checked. By the time we got back to Fort Nelson, the motor was making a helleva clatter.

We stopped at the first garage we came to and they sent us on to a Chevron station which, we were advised, was the only service station in town that worked on foreign cars. I thought that comment was somewhat odd since we were in Canada and every car there, having been made in the US or elsewhere, was in fact a foreign car! But I kept such thoughts to myself.

The mechanic at the Chevron station advised us that the VW "needed a new motor", that it would cost $300, and would take four days to install. Wanting a second opinion, we visited every other service station in Fort Nelson. No one else would even look at the engine; they all referred us to the Chevron station.

In a letter I wrote to Barbara at the time, I described the Fort Nelson of 1967 as follows:

It's cut right out of the woods surrounded by pine and birch trees with snow-capped mountains visible in the distance. There is no pavement in the entire town and no sidewalks. In front of our motel is dirt, no grass, nothing but dirt for about 150 feet. People walk down the middle of it, cars drive down it. It's like a mall. Then there's a drainage ditch, then the Alaska Highway, also dirt, then another ditch, and then another dirt mall like a big parking lot but unpaved right up to the front door of the hotel across the street. No sidewalks as I said. People walk anywhere and everywhere and cars drive any-where and everywhere, right up to the front doors of the buildings. It's like the old frontier towns in the movies, only there are no board sidewalks and all the buildings are modern. The town is about 1,000[8] people and you see every type of home from tar paper shacks to split levels, many right next to each other. There are very few cars. Almost everyone drives a pickup truck or some other type of rig. Cowboy hats are prevalent and most guys don't wear shoes. They wear cowboy boots or some other type of work boot.

Eventually a British-American dealer told us of a minister in town who had owned a couple of VWs from time to time. He called the min-ister, who offered to fix the VW for $200.

Jerry wasn't keen on putting that much money in a VW that was already six years old, especially when (in those days) you could buy a brand-new one for around $1,600. So we drove clattering around the town, visiting the various gas stations again to find out if anyone

---

[8] I found out later that Fort Nelson had some 3,000 people.

had another car or truck for sale, or if they wanted to buy the VW as she was.

We found one guy who had a 1960 Pontiac for sale. He wanted $850 for it and brought it around so we could "give 'er a test ride." When he pulled up to us and got out, I noticed he didn't turn off the engine. I was suspicious and so when I got in behind the wheel, I shut off the ignition. When I then tried to restart the car, it wouldn't start.

"Why'd you shut her off?" the man grumbled, obviously unhappy that we had learned he was trying to sell us a lemon. When he couldn't restart the Pontiac himself, he had to have it towed back to wherever he had come from.

Then we found a 1957 Ford pickup for sale for only $350. Jerry was all set to buy it from the owner of one of the gas stations, figuring we would get a tow bar, tow the VW into Anchorage, and sell one or both vehicles there. Just before we were to close the deal, a little old man who worked for the owner of the truck sidled up to us. Out of the corner of his mouth he whispered "Keep away from it! Don't say nothing 'bout me telling you this, but don't buy it!"

The old man obviously knew something was wrong with the truck and was risking his job to tip us off. We beat a hasty retreat, telling the truck owner that we'd have to think it over.

The only other car in town for sale was a 1954 Chevy for $30 but the guy who owned it had taken it fishing, and he wouldn't be back until dark.

We surely didn't know what to do. We checked the bus lines. It would have cost us $68 per person to go to Anchorage and we could take only 40 pounds of luggage per person. That meant we would have to abandon most of our gear. I had only $110 in my pocket at the time and wondered, if we abandoned the car and most of our gear, what I would do for money if and when I got to Anchorage.

We checked the freight lines. One trucking company had an empty truck going to Whitehorse where there was a Volkswagen dealer. They offered to haul the VW there so we could get it fixed. They offered a special rate of "only a dollar a mile" Since it was some 700 miles to Whitehorse, we quickly declined their kind offer.

Finally, we went to see the preacher who had offered to fix the car for $200. We talked to him and asked him if he wanted to buy the VW, but he told us he couldn't give us more than $150-$200 for it. We explained about looking for a car to tow the VW, about considering the bus, and that we couldn't see sticking a lot of money that we really didn't have into an old car.

The preacher, Dan Jespersen, was the pastor of the Fort Nelson Alliance Church. The church was in an old military barracks. Dan, his wife, and their infant son lived in a small house in back of the church. The church had a congregation of only seven or eight families at the time and, to survive, Dan worked part-time as a bag boy in the grocery store.

Dan listened to our tale of woe and to the noises coming from the car's engine. He must have taken pity on us because he again said he thought he could help. He had a book in his parish library entitled "*How to Fix Your Volkswagen*" and, if we were willing to assist, he would take the Volkswagen engine apart, see what was the matter, order new parts over the telephone from the garage in Whitehorse, and "have them shipped to us on the mail plane." Dan figured he knew what was wrong with our car, and he estimated he could repair it with around $70 worth of new parts. If we were successful, Dan said he would charge us the cost of the parts and $25 for his labor. We told him to go ahead.

For the next five or six days we worked on the car by day. I'm a guy who has trouble setting an alarm clock and yet, there I was, up to my elbows in grease and oil. It was a good thing somebody like Dan was there who knew what we were supposed to do.

After we spent two nights paying for a motel room, Dan invited us to sleep in the church at night. My dad said later that Jerry Shimek's father was fearful of our camping out because he thought we might get eaten by wolves or bears. But instead of a tent, here we were, sleeping in a church. Jerry's dad need not have worried.

Dan and his wife fed us moose-burgers and berry pie. After the engine was torn down, the new parts were ordered. They were to come in on the Saturday mail plane. "When the parts arrive on Saturday, we'll have to hustle," said Dan. "If we can't get the car put together by Saturday night, you guys are here until Monday … because I'm a preacher and I don't do manual labor on Sunday."

When the parts arrived via mail plane on Saturday morning they were, of course, the wrong parts. So we ended up spending the weekend at Fort Nelson. I went to church twice on that Sunday morning, once to Dan's church and the second time to Mass at the Catholic church. After services, Dan showed us around the town. There wasn't much to see but we appreciated his effort at hospitality. Dan's church also held services on Sunday evenings, and we felt obligated to attend that night. Going to church three times in one day seemed a bit much, but we did it.

When the right parts arrived on Monday, we put them in the VW and, surprisingly enough, the car ran. But it had no power. It needed timing, and we got one of the local garages to time the engine for us on Tuesday morning.

When it came time to square up with Dan, he apologized to us. The parts had cost more than he thought they would. Since the total parts bill was $120 rather than $70, Dan said we did not have to pay him anything!

We, of course, disagreed. We gladly paid the parts bill, and slipped Dan $50 rather than the $25 he had asked for originally, and headed, once more, for Alaska.

The VW ran, but it had problems. Somehow, in reassembling the engine, we had goofed up the wiring. Every time we turned the VW's lights on, the engine shut off. With the long daylight of the northern latitudes during the early part of the summer, that posed no problem[9].

Back on the road to Alaska after our adventures in Fort Nelson, the weather became miserable. It rained and rained, causing the road to become greasy. We actually drove above the clouds for many miles through rain, hail, and mud. Some of the hills we had to take in second gear at 20 miles-per-hour even with a four speed transmission. Even so, it was beautiful country and I saw my first snow-covered mountain. I knew, then, that I had made the right decision and there was no turning back; once I graduated, I would spend the rest of my life near such beautiful mountains.

At our campsite at Liard Hot Springs that night, we had a moose in the lake only 20 feet in front of us. Each day we saw sheep, many standing alongside the road less than thirty feet away.

We stopped briefly in Whitehorse and then it was back on the road. I thought about the alarmists who expressed concern about the so-called population explosion. They could not have ever seen this part of the world! Gas stations were 25-50 miles apart. On the Alcan, towns were 100-300 miles apart. And there was nothing in between but unpopulated beauty! It was God's imagination run wild.

Towards evening the St. Elias Range came into view. The St. Elias mountains were breathtaking and I truly believed that there could not be any more beautiful place in the world; certainly none that I had seen up to that time!

---

[9] But returning to Milwaukee in the fall, we spent a lot of time driving the Alaska highway in the dark. Once it got dark, whenever we saw another car approach we had to turn on the headlights and the engine would die. We'd then coast past the other driver, turn off the lights, and the engine would restart.

That night, from the front door of our motel-hotel in Haines Junction, Mile 1016 of the Alcan Highway, the snow-capped St. Elias mountains looked close enough to touch. Some of the peaks were as high as 18,000 feet. When I wrote my evening letter to Barbara I told her that "words cannot describe the country and scenery."

The next morning we left Haines Junction and continued through the Yukon Territory towards Alaska. The area around Kluane Lake was particularly beautiful although there was still ice on the lake in places.

Late in the afternoon we reached the Yukon-Alaska Border! We each took the other's picture at the "Welcome to Alaska" sign. We had driven some 3,700 miles, 1,200 of which were gravel, to reach this spot. We had actually made it to Alaska!

Chapter 17
My First Taste of Alaska

We were excited to be in Alaska and decided we'd drive straight on into Anchorage. There were low clouds all the way. Because of the clouds we didn't get to see the Wrangell Mountains, so the most beautiful part of the trip started about Milepost 130 of the Glenn Highway. The Glenn twists between the Chugach and Talkeetna Mountains and has to be one of the most scenic highways in America, if not the world. If such scenery existed in the Lower 48, it would have been designated a national park!

We pulled into Anchorage around 2 AM on Friday, 16 June 1967, and rented a "room" at the Palace Hotel. Although the hotel called it a "room" it was really a closet in which there were two cots along opposite walls, with about two feet of space between them. There was just enough of the room to close the door, with about three feet of space at the end of each cot. The room cost $8 a night. The desk clerk, however, suggested that we could save money if we booked the room for a week. The weekly rate was $49 or $7 a night. After paying first, and seeing the room second, we decided one night there was all we could stand.

The next morning we checked out and the clerk again suggested that we reserve the room for a week. We felt we could do better, however, thanked him, and left the hotel. We later found we should have listened to the man.

Alaska in 1967 was celebrating the Alaska Purchase Centennial, commemorating the 1867 purchase of Alaska from Russia. Anchorage was crowded with tourists because of the celebration. Jerry and I spent that first full day in Anchorage looking for a place to stay for the summer. We bought a newspaper and checked the ads but found that any places listed as available to rent were snapped up as soon as the paper hit the street. That evening we went back to the Palace Hotel. The desk clerk grinned at us. "I knew you'd be back!" he sneered smugly. "Your room tonight will cost you $12 and if you want to rent it for a week the rate is $81."

We could see that we were being cheated and we were not about to let that happen. When our cajoling and even protests did no good, we left the Palace and pitched a tent at Russian Jack Springs campground on the then far outskirts of Anchorage.

I visited the Alaska Bar Association office the next day and was invited (and treated) to a Bar Association lunch by an amiable fellow named John Havelock. In a letter to Barbara written 17 June 1967, I described Anchorage as:

> … a very clean town and quite nice. It has an international flavor and seems friendly so far. I am to attend a Bar Association luncheon on Monday as a guest of one of the other attorneys, a John Havelock, who is chairman of admissions to the Alaska Bar Association. He says he will introduce me to the other attorneys. Nice, eh?

John Havelock later became Alaska's attorney general. I have often thanked him for being the first person to buy me lunch in Alaska.

When word got around that I was looking for a summer job, I got a tip about an attorney who might have something available.

David J. Pree had his office on the second floor of the Australaska Building on the corner of Fourth and K, right across the street from the courthouse. He had a secretary, a waiting room, a small office for himself, and a library/conference room. He offered me $125 per week to clerk for him that summer.

A hundred and twenty-five dollars a week was big money! In those days law students in Milwaukee might have killed for a summer job paying $80 a week, and here I would be earning the equivalent of more than $6,000 a year! Of course I would not be working a year; only eight to ten weeks, but I quickly accepted Dave's offer. I had my first job in Alaska!

I got my first job in Alaska as a law clerk for attorney Dave Pree (1967).

Jerry found work driving a sightseeing bus for American Sightseeing Company. American Sightseeing had its office in the Captain Cook Hotel, diagonally across the street from where I would be working. While I would be getting $500 a month as a law clerk, Jerry would be making $700 a month as a bus driver. Several weeks later, the bus drivers went on strike for greater wages. Jerry refused to strike; he wanted money for tuition, and so Jerry kept working. As a result, American Sightseeing appointed Jerry its Anchorage manager. After working only two to three weeks, Jerry was now earning $900 per month and was boss of the entire company's Anchorage operation.

———

We continued to have problems finding a place to stay. The prices in Anchorage for rooms or apartments seemed outrageous. A nice apartment started around $180 per month. Perhaps because of the

Centennial, many rentals had only daily or weekly rates. We continued to camp at Russian Jack and later we camped a long way outside of town at the Eagle River Campground. After I had worked for only a few days, Dave Pree began to comment that his office smelled like campfire smoke. I realized that Jerry and I simply had to find something better than a tent and campfire. The first really available housing we found was a nice suite at the Voyager Hotel, a block from the courthouse. Unfortunately the suite was $140 a week ($160 if we wanted kitchen privileges). That kind of rent was far too expensive for somebody like me who was earning $125 a week. Thus, within seventy-two hours of thinking I was getting all the money in the world, I came face to face with economic reality. One hundred twenty-five dollars a week was *not* a lot of money in Anchorage, Alaska in 1967!

So we kept looking.

On Sunday morning I went to mass at the cathedral while Jerry walked around town. On the corner of Third and L, right at the curve, was a little yellow house with a sign that said "Room For Rent." "Let's go look at it," Jerry suggested.

The yellow house was owned by Chet and Virginia Paulk. The room was in the basement. To get to it, we went down the back stairs, into an unfinished basement. In that basement, near the front of the house, there was a small room that had been sheet-rocked. It had a double bed and a cot. On one wall there was a large picture window which looked out onto the concrete block wall of another part of the basement. I never did find out why that window was there. We had no view nor even any outside light because we were below ground. Chet wanted $20 ($10 apiece) for the room, payable weekly, and we had "kitchen privileges". We gladly accepted Chet's offer, and paid him a week's rent. Jerry and I then flipped a coin and I won; I got the double bed and Jerry got the cot.

Chet showed us the "bathroom" which consisted of a toilet that was somewhat screened in another part of the basement. The "shower" consisted of a wooden platform raised about six inches above the concrete floor with a hose mounted from a ceiling rafter. The hose was connected to the faucet in a stationary sink. No daylight was visible in that part of the basement either.

We later found out that there were another five or six fellas living in various parts of the basement. One lived behind a curtain. Another lived in the fruit cellar. We seldom saw them, but each one was paying Chet $10 to $20 a week.

At night we could hear rats scurrying above our heads in the false ceiling. I loaded my .45 with birdshot loads and placed it on my bedside table at night. Although we never saw the rats and I never had to use my revolver, we began calling our basement room at the Paulks' "the black hole of Calcutta."

––––––

One Sunday morning I decided to sleep in and then go to noon mass. About eleven in the morning the phone rang and it was Jerry. He had gone to work at 7 AM. Jerry advised that he was one driver short and he had to run a tour out to Alyeska Ski Resort and Portage Glacier. He wanted to know if I could help him out. I had never driven a bus, but I had driven dump trucks and postal vans so I agreed to the assignment. I had never been to either Alyeska or Portage but Jerry gave me a map which I studied carefully. I realized it would be a wee bit embarrassing if I, as a tour guide, got lost in front of a bunch of tourists.

"What if I get asked some questions?" I enquired of Jerry. "Just answer them," Jerry instructed. "Make something up if you don't know the right answer! They're tourists. They won't know any better!"

So 11:30 AM that Sunday morning found me driving a big bus, with twenty-five tourists, out to those two places. The tour bus was not like the tour buses of today. It was a 1941 GMC diesel with what we called a "crash box" transmission. That meant that none of the gears were synchronized. I had to double clutch every time I wanted to shift gears. There was no air-conditioning, the bus engine was loud, and there was no microphone, so I had to shout at the passengers and they had to shout at me.

One passenger asked me what kind of berries were those on the side of the road. How the hell should I know? I didn't even see any berries on the side of the road; I was too busy watching the road itself! "Those are salmon berries!" I guessed. "What's the name of that mountain?" another asked. "Mount Anderson. 4283 feet high!" I lied. I certainly could not tell those folks that they had probably been in Alaska longer than I had.

When I got to Mount Alyeska, a large ski area south of Anchorage, I got a free meal at the café, and a free ride up the chairlift.

Portage is one of the most-visited spots in Alaska. People go there to see the glaciers. I had never seen a glacier up close. We were gathered in a group gazing in fascination at Portage Glacier when one of my passengers asked me, "Why is a glacier blue?" I had no idea. So I gave an explanation that went something like this:

> A glacier is formed when snow falls in the mountains and accumulates to a depth of about forty feet. The weight of the snow compresses the lower layers, which turn to ice. The weight also forces the oxygen out of the ice and such ice with little oxygen reflects only the blue light of the spectrum.

I figured, if you can't impress them with your brilliance, baffle them with your B.S.

Apparently not quite convinced of the veracity of my answer, the passenger then said to a ranger who was standing nearby: "C'mon … tell us really why the glacier is blue!"

"We paint them once a week!" the ranger replied.

When the ranger didn't get much of a laugh, he continued:

> Actually, a glacier is formed when snow falls in the mountains and accumulates to a depth of about forty feet. The weight of the snow compresses the lower layers which turn to ice. The weight also forces the oxygen out of the ice and such ice with little oxygen reflects only the blue light of the spectrum!

He had quoted me word for word! To this day, I don't know if I guessed right in giving my answer or if the ranger simply quoted me because he didn't know the answer either.

I must have done something to please my tour bus passengers, however, because, at the end of the trip, in addition to the $25 I got paid from American Sightseeing, the passengers gave me $7.10 in tips!

Jerry still needed more drivers and since I was clerking during the week, Jerry hired our landlord, Chet Paulk.

The first day as a tour bus driver Chet stalled the bus on the railroad tracks near Portage. The passengers' concerns were not allayed when Chet turned to them and announced: "Don't worry folks! Only one train runs along this track at a time!"

Jerry took Chet off the Alyeska-Portage run and assigned him to take a busload of tourists to the Matanuska Valley, a farming area north of Anchorage. That afternoon Jerry called me at work and asked if I could get off early and take a trip north with him. Chet had driven the bus full of passengers off the road and tipped it over, and we had to go investigate.

When we got to the bus, it lay on its side in the ditch. Nobody was around. After some searching, we found Chet and the passengers in a bar at a nearby lodge. Chet was regaling the passengers with stories and urging them to "Drink up! The company is buying the drinks today!"

From what we learned later, Chet was driving the bus down a gravel road, which had soft shoulders. Chet got too close to the edge of the road, the shoulder gave way, and the bus went into the ditch, remaining upright on its wheels. "Then everybody started screaming!" Chet explained. "If they had remained seated, everything would have been fine, but when they all got up to evacuate the bus, the center of gravity shifted, causing the bus to tip over."

"It wasn't my fault!" Chet continued. "I told them to remain seated." Then, looking at the bus in the ditch, he asked innocently: "Where do you want me to drive the bus tomorrow?"

Jerry explained to Chet that he was fired. I figured we'd be evicted and have to find a different place to rent but Chet took his firing in stride. And he stayed my good friend until the day he died.

———

Meanwhile I was getting to know Anchorage better. On 22 June I wrote Barbara:

Everything is priced high here. You can't get a hamburger or cheeseburger anywhere for less than $1.35 but on the whole, for that price, they fill your plate up pretty good. I guess people get hungry in the North. I've been told by the assistant city attorney here that state jobs for attorneys in Alaska are going without any takers since they "only" pay $15,000 a year and no attorney who has been here more than a year or two wants to take such a "low paying" job. From what I've been able to find out, winters here are about the same as Milwaukee, but not as damp a cold. The annual precipitation here is less (than Milwaukee) ... The boss took my office key away from me today. He said I should have more free time and that the office hours are from nine to five. That there is no need for me to come in before he does or stay later. That I need more time for recreation and relaxation. That he made the same mistake of putting in too many hours when he was my age.

On 26 June I wrote Barbara more of my impressions about Anchorage:

It has real people who are not out to impress someone. It has fresh air. It has no parking problems as yet and no traffic jams. It has a "good pace" instead of a "rat race". It allows time for living instead of "making a living". It allows one to see the majesty of God (in the mountains, ocean, streams, and woods) instead of the "greatness of man". It provides room for a person to be an individual and not a number or a cog in the wheel of progress. It provides enough civilization for a man to feel pride in himself and enough wildness for him to feel dependency on God … It is where I want to "live" … instead of "exist" as would be the appropriate (word) for Milwaukee.

I had been in Anchorage less than two weeks and the city was already starting to grow on me!

———

On the Fourth of July, Jerry had to work so he let me take the car back to Portage Glacier. Having visited the place once in the tour bus, I wanted to explore it more closely. That night I wrote Barbara the following:

(Portage Glacier) is a pretty fantastic sight. You stand at one end of a huge blue lake. At the other end is a tall mountain of black rock sheathed in translucent blue ice, the ice in the shape of a large bobsled run, though narrower at the top than it is at the bottom. At the end of this huge slope of ice, which is almost a mile wide, is a perpendicular drop of what I would guess to be several hundred feet, to the lake itself. Chunks of ice break off this edge or perpendicular ice wall, and splash into the lake where they float around like icebergs. The air temperature was about 65 (degrees) but all I could see was ice and rock.[10]

In the morning it was cloudy and the ice took on almost a sky-blue hue, so bright that it almost hurt your eyes. Of course I had no film for my camera, but Jerry and I will go there again and at that time I'll send you pictures. It was one of the most fantastic

---

[10] Portage Glacier has receded so that it is no longer visible from where I wrote that note to Barbara some forty years ago.

scenes I have ever witnessed. This, the largest glacier in the area, though by no means the largest in the state, was inaccessible by car or foot, but up a canyon to one side about a mile and a half, was another smaller glacier[11]. I wanted to see one of these babies up close so I hiked up there, in places having to wade glacial streams caused by the melting of the ice. Near the head of the canyon was a large snow field, which I had to go over. The snow must have piled up there for centuries as this particular pile was about a quarter of a mile long and about fifty feet deep, but of course it was packed hard so I didn't sink when I went over. On the other side of the snowfield was an open space of a block piled high with jumbles of rocks, and the face of the glacier itself, also this mysterious blue color. In the face of the glacier were two ice caves caused by the ice melting, and the glacial streams I mentioned before came rushing out of the dark translucent blue of these caves. The water then rushed down the canyon, disappearing for a time under the snow-field, to reappear on the other side, where it continued its head-long dash into the valley and its blue, iceberged lake.

Beautiful is not the (adequate) word for it. I sat down on this jumbled pile of rocks between the glacier's face and the snowfield and just gaped. On two sides were the high rocky, moss-covered slopes of the canyon walls; behind me was the snowfield and in front was this enormous hunk of ice extending hundreds of feet up the slope of the mountain that gave it birth. It is then that you realize the grandeur of God and the puniness of man. I ate lunch at that spot and after, smoked a seegar …

———

On weekends I tried to get out into the wild as much as possible. One Saturday I drove to Bonnie Lake, at about Mile 82 of the Glenn Highway. I grabbed my fishing pole and started working my way down a stream running out of the lake. I ran into another fellow who was fishing. "What kind of gun is that you are wearing?" he asked.

I told him it was a Smith & Wesson .22 revolver.

"Kind of small, isn't it?" he asked.

---

[11] Byron Glacier.

I told him that I didn't think I needed anything bigger than a .22 because there seemed to be a lot of people at the lake, so I was sure there weren't any bears in the area.

"Oh, yeah?" he replied. Pointing to the stream along which we were standing, he told me that a fellow camper had killed a grizzly bear at that very spot the day before "after the bear came charging out of the woods and across the stream at him!"

I thought a bit about carrying a bigger gun but the following week saw me at Hatcher Pass with another of Chet's tenants, a guy named Pete Durney. (Pete later became an attorney also and, last I heard, practices in Colorado.) Pete and I had decided to climb Bullion Mountain on the backside ridgeline from the old Independence Mine. Since the area was above tree line and I could see for miles, I again carried the .22 S&W figuring that there was no place around for a bear to hide.

We had just hiked over the military crest of the mountain when Pete spotted a grizzly several hundred yards away. Luckily, the bear did not spot us. I realized then that bears are where you find them in Alaska and I've never exclusively carried a pistol that small again.

———

On 24 July I wrote Barbara:

> You asked why I want to live in Alaska. I'll try and tell you briefly—I like freedom, and in the wild places here I feel unrestrained. I like solitude, and here it is attainable. I like an unhurried pace of life, and not the "rat race" type of existence found in Milwaukee. I like the mountains, trees, and ever flowing water. I like the abundant wildlife. I like the clear fresh air. I like to feel a part of something that is growing, and not stagnating like Milwaukee. I feel closer to God here.

Actually I wrote Barbara a lot that summer. Kids communicate nowadays on the Internet. Our Internet then was the US Mail. I probably wrote Barbara daily and she wrote me back the same way. I got to know her better during our correspondence and she got to know me better too. Our letters were full of speculation as to whether we would have a future together in Alaska and we looked forward to seeing each other in the fall to further explore our relationship.

One evening I was working late at Dave Pree's office when I got a phone call. It was Barbara. She told me for the first time, in that call, that she loved me! She had gone to dinner with my dad and my sister Carol, and later Barbara and Carol went out on the town. Barbara said she and my sister were having drinks with a couple of football players they had met when she decided that "I suddenly realized that I loved you and since I couldn't be with the guy I loved, I ought to go home."

And so she went home and phoned me. We talked for quite a while. I knew then that there was a good chance that when I returned to Alaska after graduation, I would not be coming alone.

———

I wrote my dad a few letters also, and he and I talked on the phone at least weekly. Dad didn't need much convincing when I suggested he come and see Alaska. In August of that year Dad, and his buddy John Schaff flew to Alaska. Jerry and I picked them up at the airport in an American Sightseeing bus. Dad and John got a kick out of that. I spent a number of days, when I wasn't working, showing Dad the sights around Anchorage.

Dad said he wanted to see the "Manatuska Valley" where, in the thirties, a number of Wisconsin residents were settled by the government to get a new start in farming.

I told dad it was pronounced "Matanuska," not "Manatuska."

Dad, however, continued to call it Manatuska for reasons I could not guess. After Dad died, however, I inherited an old encyclopedia set that he had owned. In the encyclopedia it referred to the Alaska farming area as the Manatuska Valley. I've never seen it called that anywhere else.

Dad really liked Alaska and wanted to see even more of it. We planned a trip to Fairbanks but Fairbanks had a big flood that year. As a result, Dad and John took me on an Alaska Airlines Golden Nugget flight to Nome, with stops in Unalakleet and Kotzebue. At one of the stops, before we got to Nome, Alaska Airlines loaned each passenger a nice parka to wear.

I found out why the airline was so nice when I got to Nome. While on the main street I visited the old "Board of Trade" bar in Nome. Allegedly the bar had been established by Wyatt Earp of Tombstone, Arizona fame. While wearing my tourist parka, I ordered a beer. That beer cost me $2.50! A guy next to me, who had no parka, also ordered a beer. It cost him only a dollar! I found out later that the tourists with colorful parkas were referred to as "Easter Eggs" by the locals.

I quickly scurried back to our hotel and ditched the parka. Without the parka I, too, was able to buy beer for a buck!

My dad (right) and I on the beach at Nome, Alaska with our Alaska Airlines "Easter Egg" coats (1967). The locals knew we were tourist because of these coats and charged us more for drinks at the local saloons.

On August 19th I wrote Barbara:

At this moment I am writing from the lobby of a hotel built on the golden sands of the beach here at Nome, Alaska. Behind me is the Bering Sea, stretching all the way to Siberia 146 miles away. I've seen some fabulous things today ... Eskimos, fish drying in the sun, gold, fur, ivory, Eskimo dances, walrus skin boats called "oomiaks," skin kayaks, mastodon tusks, a dog team pulling a dog sled, huskies, malamutes, and a gold dredge.

The city of Nome is wooden sidewalks and dirt streets. The buildings are all very weatherbeaten, ramshackle, and God knows what all else. Our hotel (the Golden Nugget) is brand-new. Flush toilets and running water. Nome has only had these modern conveniences for two to three years. At least half the city still uses "honey buckets" and has water brought in by truck.

The fact that flush toilets were a new experience for the people of Nome was shown to me quite graphically. I was in a men's room at the hotel when two little Native boys walked in. One was about nine and one was about seven. "Watch this!" the older one said to the younger. The older boy then crumpled up some toilet paper and threw it in the toilet bowl. Then he flushed the toilet. The younger boy clapped his hands in glee. "Let me try it!" he insisted. It was obvious the younger fellow had never seen a flush toilet!

My letter to Barbara continued:

> I crossed the Arctic Circle today and have a certificate to prove it. Had a Schlitz (a Milwaukee beer) in the Board of Trade Saloon tonight which is the oldest bar in the Arctic. I had reindeer meat for lunch and was it ever good. Tonight we went down to see the (King Island) Eskimo dancers. After we watched them dance, they insisted some of us try it. There are about 80 people on this tour. They picked four people at random to try and dance Eskimo style, i.e., to the beat of walrus skin drums. Guess who was one of the four? You're right. After I finished two Eskimo dances, they gave me a walrus tooth as a reward for a good job. How about that? …
>
> Right now the husky dogs are howling outside the hotel. There are more dogs than people in this town!

———

When we all got back to Anchorage from the Arctic, our summer was ending. During that summer, I had learned that my once-thought-magnificent salary didn't go very far in Anchorage. There were a number of times when, several days short of my next paycheck, I had to resort to buying a loaf of bread and a jar of peanut butter which fed me until the next payday. I'd walk down to the Park Strip and sit at a picnic table and eat my peanut butter and jelly sandwich. When we did eat out, we didn't eat at any fancy Anchorage restaurants. Once in a while we'd walk down to the Two-Ten-Two, a little café on Fifth and Barrow, to have a toasted ham and cheese sandwich with french fries. The whole meal cost $1.65. Or we'd eat at the D&D Bar on Fourth Avenue, or Peggy's Airport Café across from Merrill Field.

Once in a while we stopped for a beer after work. A glass of beer cost a quarter at the Panhandle Bar on Fourth Avenue. Jerry had, on one occasion, gone into the Montana Club to get a beer. I wasn't with him at the time but he told me afterwards what happened. "There I was ... drinking my beer ... minding my own business," Jerry said, "when there was a commotion at the front door. I looked over there and there was a great big guy nailing a sheet of plywood over the door from the outside. He was also nailing the door shut! I looked around and everybody was looking at me! And I suddenly noticed that I was the only Caucasian guy in the place. I quickly ducked in the mens' room in back, got up on the commode, and jumped out of the window into the alley. I have no idea why the guy was nailing the door shut but I didn't wait around to find out!"

———

It was soon time for Jerry and me to start getting ready to drive back to Wisconsin. "Before we drive out of here, let's take Chet and Virginia out to dinner," Jerry suggested. "You can take your boss, your dad, and Mr. Schaff too! You know ... kind of a way of showing our appreciation!" I thought it was a good idea but I expressed my concern about the cost. "We'll take them out for Chinese food!" Jerry suggested. "We can go to some Oriental joint and get chop suey, and even fortune cookies, for two or two and a half bucks a plate!"

Mom had cooked chop suey once or twice at home but, as a kid from Milwaukee, I had never been to a real Chinese restaurant, or to any other Oriental joint, for that matter. So I let Jerry make the reservations while I took on the task of inviting everyone.

Jerry made reservations at a place called Nikko Gardens. Nikko Gardens was out on the way to the airport and certainly was not "some Oriental joint." Although we didn't know it at the time, Nikko Gardens was one of the finest Japanese restaurants in Anchorage.[12]

When we got to the restaurant, we had quite a group of people: Jerry's mom and dad, who had come to Anchorage to see their son; Chet Paulk and his wife, our landlords; my employer Dave Pree and his wife Nadine; my dad and his buddy John; and, of course, Jerry and I. "The restaurant even gave us a private room!" Jerry exulted.

---

[12] Nikko Gardens burned down many years ago but old-time Alaskans still speak about it fondly.

When we got the menu, however, I knew we were in serious trouble. There was no chop suey listed at two or two and a half dollars a plate. In fact, there was no chop suey listed at all. Nor was there anything else on that menu for two or two and a half dollars a plate. In fact there wasn't anything on there even close to twice that price!

Dave Pree, who had once visited Japan, ordered sake and a variety of appetizers. We had two lovely Japanese waitresses serving us. It was a wonderful meal.

The bill came to One Hundred and Fifteen bucks! I had fifty dollars cash in my pocket and Jerry had forty dollars. Thank goodness it was on a Friday and I had just gotten my paycheck. I got a ten-dollar bill from Jerry and endorsed my entire paycheck over to the restaurant. That dinner at Nikko Gardens had cost me one tenth of my entire summer wages! And while I didn't get chop suey that night, nor have I ever eaten chop suey since, I developed a taste for Japanese food that is with me to this day.

———

On my last day of work at Dave Pree's office he told me that he was expecting me to come to work for him when I returned to Alaska the next summer. He said I'd make a good attorney but that I just "needed a little polish."

I wrote my last letter to Barbara from Anchorage on 23 August and at 5 AM the next day we left Anchorage to return to Milwaukee and real life.

On the way out of town we stopped for gas. A guy pulled up to us in a Model A Ford. I told Jerry that a classmate of mine in high school had driven a car just like that one. The driver of the Model A got out and it *was* my high school classmate, Steve Gross. We visited for a short time and then went our separate ways. I hadn't seen Steve since high school in 1960. And I haven't seen or heard from him since that August day in 1967, when two guys from Milwaukee happened to meet again, buying gas at the same time and place in Anchorage, Alaska.

The drive back to Milwaukee filled me with mixed emotions. I truly hated to leave Alaska but I really was anticipating seeing Barbara again. She intrigued me a lot and I wanted to see if we had a future together.

In the Yukon we saw a man killed on the Alcan Highway. He evidently rolled his pickup truck and was thrown out. The truck rolled on top of him. We got there right after it happened but there was nothing anyone could do for him.

We stopped in Fort Nelson to see Dan Jespersen[13] and then pushed on.

It was clear that the VW was on its last legs. By the time we got to Interstate 94 heading east through North Dakota, the VW would not go more than thirty-two miles per hour, even when the accelerator was on the floorboard. The minimum speed on that highway was forty-five miles an hour which was far faster than we could go. So we'd putt along at thirty-two miles per hour until we were passed by a semi. Then we'd quickly duck into his slipstream and get sucked along at whatever speed the truck was traveling. Eventually the trucker would get angry at that little VW tail-gating him and the trucker would pull over. We'd then putt past him at thirty-two miles-per- hour until the next truck came along.

We finally reached Milwaukee on 31 August 1967 at 2:30 AM. My first taste of Alaska was over but I vowed to go back for more!

---

[13] I lost touch with Dan Jesperson after that return trip through Fort Nelson. I tried to contact Dan several times without success until finally, in 1982 while in British Columbia, I got his phone number and called him. We renewed old acquaintances and have kept in touch, at Christmas, ever since.

Several years ago, Dan called me and told me that he had hoped to visit us when his church voted to send him to the Billy Graham Crusade in Anchorage. He had planned to surprise us but, unfortunately, the church couldn't raise the money for him to come. Still, Dan said, he hoped to make it to Alaska eventually.

After talking to Barbara, we sent Dan the money to come to the Billy Graham crusade in Alaska. As Barbara put it, "He helped you get to Alaska. The least we can do is to help him get here!"

When Dan arrived here, he asked what he could do to repay us for paying his way to Anchorage. I told Dan that I was only repaying him for all that he had done for me that long ago summer when he helped me get to Alaska. "Say a couple prayers for me at the Billy Graham Crusade!" I told him. "Even though I'm a Catholic boy, it doesn't hurt to have all of my bases covered!"

Chapter 18
The Longest Year

I returned to Wisconsin from Alaska on the last day of August 1967. I first went home and saw Dad, and then I called Barbara. We arranged to meet later in the day. I then checked in with Cy Cybulski, the Milwaukee postmaster. He had kept his promise-my job at the post office was waiting for me.

Soon law school began. I was back to spending the day in classes, and then working five to six hours picking up mail from mail boxes and postal stations. I'd get through with work around 9 PM and then go see Barbara. She had an apartment with two other roommates near 112th off North Avenue. Since I hadn't had supper, Barbara always fixed me something to eat. Generally it was a TV dinner. It was late and I was hungry and I was with my girl. As a result, even a TV dinner tasted pretty good to me!

After eating dinner at Barbara's, I'd go home to study until midnight or 1 AM before hitting the sack. The next day the routine would start all over again.

The first thing I noticed once I returned to Milwaukee was that I couldn't see as far as I had been able to see in Alaska. There were no mountains in the distance. In fact there really wasn't any "distance" at all! I felt closed in. And the fresh air I had come to know in Alaska was gone. Instead, there was a combination of smells-yeasts from the breweries, chemicals from the tannery, cookies from the cookie factory, car and truck exhausts, and other smells best left undeciphered.

I realized it was going to be the longest year of my life until I could return home to Alaska.

——

The only thing that promised to make that year bearable was Barbara. I really looked forward to getting to know her better.

One Saturday I asked Barbara to go duck and goose hunting with me at Horicon Marsh. She went, even though it was a cold, windy, and rainy day. I don't even remember if I shot anything. I just remember that Barbara had gone on a hunt with me. She also joined me for a deer hunt later that fall.

My father suggested that I invite Barbara to come to our house for supper. Dad was a great cook and was quite proud of the asparagus he had grown in the backyard. As a side dish to the dinner, Dad proudly served asparagus tips. Barbara hated asparagus, but she still ate Dad's asparagus, telling him how great it tasted. Dad fell in love with her too.

I went to Elkhart, Indiana to meet Barbara's family. Her father had died the same year as my mom. But I still had to get approved by Barbara's mom, Barbara's two sisters, their husbands, some nieces and nephews, and several sets of grandparents, uncles, and aunts. I must have passed some sort of test. I liked every member of Barbara's family and it appeared, to me at least, that they liked me. "It's not that they like you!" Barbara explained. "It's just that they don't understand you enough not to like you!" So I settled for that.

———

After my mom had died, Dad promised me that when I decided to get engaged, I could have Mom's engagement ring. Dad had sold his 1929 Chevrolet to purchase that ring. There was just one condition-Dad had to approve of the girl before he'd give me Mom's ring. I readily agreed. After all, Dad had done a great job picking my mom so it was obvious he knew a good woman when he saw one.

Since my return from Alaska I had spent a lot of time with Barbara and she seemed interested in going to Alaska with me. She was good to me; she was good to my dad; she seemed to love me and I knew I loved her. After several months I decided to ask her to marry me. Of course I didn't expect her to turn me down. We had discussed marriage for several months. We just hadn't done anything formal to begin the proceedings.

But before I could ask Barbara to marry me, I had to get the ring from Dad. And before I could get the ring from Dad, I first I had to get his approval. When I told Dad I was thinking of asking Barbara to marry me, and wanted his approval, he told me, "If you don't ask her to marry you, I'll ask her to marry me!"

Ever thereafter, Dad treated Barbara like a beloved daughter until the day he died.

On Barbara's birthday, I popped the question and she said "Yes!"

We were going to go to Alaska together!

———

The rest of the year was somewhat of a blur. I kept studying and working and let Barbara and her sisters plan the wedding. Other than picking the groomsmen and helping with the guest list, I stayed out of the planning. "Tell me where you want me and when you want me there," was all I asked.

My family gave Barbara a wedding shower. I think they were all worried about our going to Alaska because we got envelopes with cash, and boxes of canned goods.

I still had my 1959 Buick but I hadn't been driving it for a while. To raise some money for school I had placed the Buick on my buddy's used car lot. I was asking $700 for it. In the meantime, I bought a two-tone green 1953 Chevrolet Bel Aire four door sedan. I paid $30 for it. It ran well but burned oil. I'd have to add a quart or two several times a week. The floor was rusted out on the front passenger's side and Barbara could see the street go by below her feet whenever we went out in my car. Barbara had a neat British racing-green 1965 Mustang and so, when faced with riding in my 1953 Chevy and watching the road go by under her feet, Barbara always suggested we take her Mustang when we went out. I certainly didn't mind because she always let me do the driving.

As we got closer to the time to leave for Alaska, my dad insisted that we sell our cars. As a wedding gift he bought us a brand-new bright red 1968 Chevrolet Chevelle station wagon. It had a V-8 with a stick shift and a "posi-traction" rear end. It cost $2,625 and was my first new car.

———

I had been trying to call Dave Pree in Alaska for a number of months, without success. I had sent him a number of letters keeping him informed of my progress in law school, my engagement, and my plans to leave for Alaska after graduation. I got no responses to my letters.

Two weeks before graduation Dave called me. He advised that due to personal and family problems he was not going to be able to hire me after all! Upon telling Barbara that when we got to Alaska I had no job waiting for me, she asked me what I wanted to do. I told her that I was still going to go to Alaska, I wanted her to go with me, and that I'd even sell shoes, if I had to, when I got there!

"OK. Count me in!" was her response.

———

I graduated from law school on the second of June 1968. I was admitted to the Wisconsin Bar on the third of June 1968. After I was admitted, an old neighbor lady, Mrs. Bartells, called me and congratulated me. I had delivered newspapers to her when I had my paper route and she now asked me to prepare a will for her. "I want to tell everyone that my newsboy prepared my will for me!" Mrs. Bartells explained, with a laugh. So I drafted her will and Barbara typed it up. Drafting that will was the only occasion I practiced law in Wisconsin.

Barbara and I were married on 22 June 1968 in St. Vincent's Catholic Church in Elkhart, Indiana. Dad was my best man. We had a nice reception at the Hotel Elkhart downtown.

We left for Alaska on 26 June 1968. June 1968 was a busy month and the real start of our lives as Alaskans.

Chapter 19
New Alaskans

Barbara and I shipped our personal effects, the canned goods from the wedding shower, and a dozen cartons of books to Alaska. The total expenses for shipping everything we owned to Alaska was $229.42. We loaded the rest into our new Chevelle, along with camping gear. We also put in the only piece of furniture we owned, a metal ashtray on a pedestal stand. I smoked a pipe at the time and my mentor, Leo Fendryk, gave me the ashtray as a souvenir from his law office on Milwaukee's South Side.

After saying goodbye to our families, Barbara and I headed to Alaska. That trip was our honeymoon.

We had two newly purchased sleeping bags which zipped together, so on several occasions on the way north we camped. Our best campsite was on the shores of Kluane Lake in the Yukon. It was Barbara's first experience with camping and she seemed to enjoy it. We spent a total of $79.79 on lodging, $64.13 on food, and $134.14 for gas and covered the 3,785 miles in eight days. We averaged 14.1 miles per gal. (As I write this we are in the midst of a sharp increase in the price of fuel and I suddenly realize that my most recent fill-up cost me $144.00, almost $10 more than what I spent for gasoline on that entire 1968 trip!)

We pulled into Anchorage on the Fourth of July 1968 and checked into a newly constructed motel, the Mush Inn.

———

The next day I showed Barbara Anchorage. That evening, a banker I had met the year before took us up on the hills overlooking Anchorage and told us: "This area of town is called the 'Hillside.' This is where you should build a house!" We thought the view was stunning but we sure weren't ready to build a house. Indeed, I didn't even have a job!

A few days later we found an unfurnished apartment at 221 Meyer Street in Mountain View. Our rent was $170 per month. We moved our pedestal ashtray and our sleeping bags into our first home. Our personal effects arrived a few days later.

Like most young people starting out in those days we built a bookcase out of bricks and boards and a couch out of bundles of newspapers with a blanket over the top. We bought a small unfinished circular table and four unfinished kitchen chairs, and painted them lime green to match the appliances. For several weeks we slept on sleeping bags in one of the two bedrooms until our landlord took pity on us and sold us a bed for $20. We made friends with some other couples our age who lived in the complex. Most of them were "military" since we lived near the Elmendorf Air Force Base. Some of them remain dear friends to this day.

When Barbara and I paid our first month's rent and a security deposit and purchased the few furnishings we really needed, we had about $750 left in the bank. That money, our car, and the furnishings were all we owned in the world!

———

I immediately began to look for a job. I did some contract work for an elderly-to me at least- attorney named Helen Simpson. I think she paid me $20 per hour, which I was glad to get. In those days there were only about seven women attorneys in Anchorage-women attorneys were rare. If I recall, we had only one woman in my law school graduating class.

Helen Simpson and I stayed friends until the day she died. In fact, she honored me many years later when she asked me to represent her in some aspects of closing out her practice.

But I needed to find something more substantial than contract work to support me and my new bride. Although I had told Barbara that I was willing to "sell shoes" if necessary to survive, I really wanted to practice law and so I set about to find a permanent position.

I heard that the attorney general's office was looking for attorneys. The Anchorage AG's office was, coincidentally, in the same building as Dave Pree's office, where I had worked the summer before. I met with a fellow named Dennis Marvin, who was the head man in the Anchorage

AG's office. Marvin told me that I should report back on Monday morning "ready to go to work."

I had my first job as a married man! Barbara and I were ecstatic.

I got up early that Monday, put on my new graduation suit, a white shirt, and one of my graduation ties, and grabbed my graduation briefcase Barbara's mom had given me. Barbara had purchased some legal pads for me to use in my new job and, of course, I had my graduation pen and pencil set. I kissed my new bride goodbye and set off for my new job.

When I walked in the AG's office promptly at 8 AM, I was met by a tall angular woman by the name of Kay Zumwalt. Kay was the office manager. I introduced myself and told her I was a new attorney reporting for work.

"I don't know anything about that," Kay Zumwalt replied. "Who hired you?" I told her I had been hired the week before by Mr. Marvin. "Well, I don't know anything about that!" Kay repeated. "Please have a seat in the waiting room until Mr. Marvin comes in."

I sat in the waiting room from 8 AM until around 10:30 AM. Then the phone rang and Kay Zumwalt answered it. I could only hear Kay's side of the conversation and it went something like this.

"Mr. Marvin, there's a fellow here in the waiting room who says he is an attorney who you hired last week."

"Well, he's been here since 8 AM."

"He says he is ready to go to work."

"Maybe you had better tell him that, Mr. Marvin."

"No, I think you should tell him that, Mr. Marvin."

"Very well … I'll tell him that."

The phone call then ended. Immediately thereafter, Kay Zumwalt came into the waiting room. "Mr. Marvin just called," she explained. "He says you should go home. He says he found out he doesn't have the authority to hire any attorneys at this time. He says only the attorney general himself has such authority. He says he will call you later."

I asked her how I could get in touch with the attorney general himself.

"The attorney general is G. Kent Edwards and you can't reach him until later in the week," Kay explained. "Mr. Edwards is on the East Coast on a recruiting trip, hiring some new attorneys!"

When I pointed out that I, a new attorney, was already in the office ready to go to work, Kay Zumwalt repeated, "Mr. Marvin said you should go home … He will call you later!" Kay, not Marvin, was informing me I really didn't have my first job as a married man with a wife to support!

So I went home to my new bride. I walked into the door of our apartment in my graduation suit, with my graduation tie, carrying my graduation briefcase, and had to tell my beloved Barbara I had, apparently been "fired" from my first job, after only three hours. After Dave Pree's call the previous month informing me that I didn't have a job with him, and now this, I'm sure Barbara wondered what kind of loser she had picked for her husband.

———

Over the next several days I continued to look for a job, without success. Finally Dennis Marvin called me on Thursday morning. "Can you go out to the airport with me this afternoon?" he asked. "The attorney general is coming in on a plane and I'd like him to meet you."

So after lunch I once again put on my graduation suit and a graduation tie, and drove out to the airport. I was introduced to Attorney General G. Kent Edwards as he got off the plane. Edwards said hello and I told him: "You're the first guy I've decided I dislike, even before meeting you!"

Obviously taken aback, Edwards asked me what I meant.

"Here you are … flying around the country at taxpayers' expense, looking for attorneys to hire for your office, while I'm sitting here in your Anchorage office ready to go to work … and I get sent home!" I told him. "That really pissed me off!"

"Let's go have a drink!" said AG Edwards, and we did.

At the Crow's Nest bar at the top of the Captain Cook Hotel we got down to business. I told him my background, my experience with his office, and that I was ready to go to work. I told him I hated having to return home and tell my new bride that I really hadn't been hired at all. Edwards asked some questions, seemed satisfied, and said, "Come to work on Monday. I'll pay you $1,006 per month!"

"I've changed my initial opinion of you," I told Edwards. "I'm starting to believe I like you!"

I couldn't wait to get home to Barbara to tell her that, once again, I was hired by the attorney general's office. We both could not believe my salary. My father had retired from the Prudential Insurance Company the previous year, after working for that company for thirty-five years. His salary, when he retired, was approximately $14,000 per year. Now here was I, in my first job out of law school, earning almost that much! Wow!

I worked with a lot of great attorneys at the AG's office and some, like Sanford Gibbs and Keith Brown, remain my great friends to this day.

———

Our first dinner guest as a married couple was G. Kent Edwards himself. Barbara was a bit overwhelmed when I told her that I had invited the AG for dinner, but she did her best to put on a great meal for our important guest. She did get suggestions from her mom and sisters via telephone for several days before her first dinner guest arrived.

As Barbara got more comfortable entertaining in our little apartment, I invited many folks I met who were visiting Anchorage and who, I felt, might enjoy a home-cooked meal. We had Trooper Lloyd Dubber from Sand Point, Judge Sanders from Nome, and Police Chief Ed Kliese from Unalaska, among others, as our dinner guests. We also entertained several couples who lived in our apartment complex and became lifelong friends with a number of them.

———

Alaska had a rule that an attorney from outside Alaska could practice law for a limited time while he or she prepared for and took the first bar exam. So despite the fact that I had yet to get admitted to the Alaska Bar, I could still work as an assistant attorney general.

On my first or second day on the job, I was told to accompany the state's regional sanitarian to close down a restaurant for violating standards of cleanliness. I had never heard of a regional sanitarian, nor did I know what a regional sanitarian did. But Joe Blair, the sanitarian, and I got into a state vehicle and drove high into the Talkeetna Mountains to the Independence Mine Lodge. Blair conducted his inspection of the kitchen, found sanitary violations, and signed and presented a certificate to the cook closing the place down. We then drove back to Anchorage. Before we could get into court, the lodge asked for another inspection, which it passed. Blair allowed the restaurant to reopen. No one in law school had ever told us about such summary justice.

Several days later, I was told to accompany an assistant district attorney named Russell Gallagher to Kodiak Island. Kodiak is a huge island in the Gulf of Alaska, and it is home to some of the largest brown bears in the world. I learned on that trip that Kodiak Island is also one of the best fishing places in Alaska.

Floyd Short, an Alaska Department of Fish and Game protection officer in Kodiak, had arrested a fisherman, and seized and impounded his fishing boat for "possession of undersized crabs." Short took the fisherman to jail and took the fishing boat, the *Lynn Kendall*, and tied it up alongside the dock in the Kodiak boat harbor. The last thing the *Kendall's* skipper said, as he was led off to jail, was "I hope the damned thing sinks! I'll sue the state for a million dollars!"

That night the *Lynn Kendall* sank, and started leaking diesel fuel into the Kodiak boat harbor. The City of Kodiak filed a lawsuit against the State of Alaska demanding that the state do something about the sunken boat and the fuel spill, and so Russell Gallagher and I were sent to Kodiak to negotiate a contract to raise the boat. We were accompanied by Captain Bob Logan, a marine surveyor.

Our flight to Kodiak was on a Constellation, a large four-engine propeller airplane known as a Connie. We were told when we reached Kodiak our flight had been the very last scheduled passenger flight of a Connie in the United States.

Gallagher, Logan, and I went to the boat harbor, looked at the *Kendall*, talked to Floyd Short, had dinner, and then checked into the old Kodiak Hotel. It was so old that it was torn down several months later. Gallagher went to visit his folks, who lived in Kodiak, while Logan ("Captain Bob" we called him) and I walked around the town. I thought: "Here I am, in Alaska less than three weeks, and walking around Kodiak, a place I had only read about! And I was paid to come here, and I'm being paid to stay here tonight! It can't get much better than this!"

I was wrong. It got even better!

The next morning Gallagher and I got together with some folks from the Bechtel Corporation and arranged to have them raise the *Lynn Kendall*. Gallagher did most of the legal work. I had never seen a salvage contract much less negotiated one, so it was a good learning experience for me. We finished our work shortly before noon, and then I was invited to have lunch with Gallagher's parents. Gallagher's mom was much taller than her husband and kept talking about how many fish she had caught recently. Somehow, I managed to persuade her to take me fishing that afternoon since we had a number of hours before Russ and I had to fly back to Anchorage.

Mrs. Gallagher drove me "out the road system," as they say in Kodiak, and several miles out of town she pulled over and parked. We grabbed some fishing poles out of her vehicle and headed into the woods. After a short walk "busting brush" we came to a small pool of water. The pool was about twenty yards in diameter and was simply filled with silver salmon. One cast and my line tickled the backs of eight or ten fish. One cast and I had a fish on. And if that fish managed to throw the hook, another fish would go after my lure before I could retrieve it further. I literally caught ten- to fifteen-pound silver salmon on every cast! Once we got our limits, which took only a few minutes, we fished "catch and release" until my arms got tired. I had never seen such fishing in my life! Later that day, when Russ Gallagher and I flew back to Anchorage, part of my checked baggage consisted of a cooler full of fresh salmon fillets.

Bechtel raised the *Lynn Kendall* under Logan's careful eye. Captain Bob determined that the *Kendall* had sunk because somebody had opened the sea cocks, allowing seawater to flood the boat. There had been no overnight watchman on the boat and the *Kendall's* skipper had been released from jail only several hours before the boat sank. And true to his promise, after the *Kendall* sank-or was sunk-its skipper sued the state for a million dollars. The case was still pending when I left the Department of Law and I offered to continue working on the case on an hourly basis but my offer was declined. Eventually the state paid the skipper of the *Lynn Kendall* $180,000! I like to think that if I had been allowed to continue working that case, the *Kendall's* skipper would have ended up paying the State of Alaska!

———

Another case I recall working on involved a guide named Al Burnette. Somehow Burnette was chosen to guide the King of Nepal on a sheep hunt. If I recall, the king was given a special permit to take a sheep in the Knik Glacier area. The king had a retinue of attendants and even ferried in crates of china and silverware from the Captain Cook Hotel to the hunting area. There was quite a camp set up with huge tents, tables, and chairs. Everything was first class. Apparently Burnette was being urged by the state to make sure the king had a good Alaskan experience so, to ensure the king got his sheep, Burnette allegedly hired a helicopter to drive some Dall sheep down to where the king waited in ambush, rifle in hand. The king got a sheep and left Alaska with good memories. Burnette got a criminal citation and a court date. I remember thinking that somebody high in the administration was covering his behind at Burnette's expense.

———

My very first trial was a life-changing event. Dennis Marvin assigned me a case involving a doctor, in his forties, who had flown to Alaska with the doctor's eighteen-year-old mistress and the doctor's fifteen-year-old son. The doctor left his wife of many years stewing in Colorado.

Once in Alaska, the doctor and his mistress applied to the state to adopt a baby. The doctor and his mistress signed an affidavit saying that they were "husband and wife" and the adoption was granted. Meanwhile, the doctor's wife commenced and pursued a very nasty divorce case in Colorado.

Since the adoption was clearly accomplished by fraud, my job was to get the adoption set aside. A hearing was set before Family Court Judge Harold Butcher.

The doctor retained an attorney named Edgar Paul Boyko. Ed Boyko was considered one of the best attorneys in the state of Alaska. His nickname was "The Snow Tiger" and he was a force to be reckoned with. I, of course, had never heard of him.

Boyko had been born in Vienna a month after World War I ended. He had attended the University of Vienna in Austria, the University of St. Andrew in Scotland, the University of Maryland, and others. He was admitted to the bar in Maryland, the District of Columbia, California, and Alaska. He first came to Alaska in 1953 from California but continued to maintain offices in both states. Shortly after our trial, Boyko replaced Kent Edwards as attorney general.

As I said, I had never heard of Edgar Paul Boyko. That was probably a good thing. Had I known of him I would probably have been scared to death to face such an opponent in what would be my first court trial.

I left my office on the morning of the hearing and told Kay Zumwalt that I would be back before lunch. After all, I had a certified copy of the divorce complaint filed by the doctor's wife saying she and the doctor were married at the time the doctor and his paramour signed their affidavit. I also had the wife standing by, via telephone, ready to testify to that fact. And I had the notary who witnessed the doctor and his girlfriend sign the affidavit. From my three years of law school training, I knew there was no way I could lose!

After the trial was over, I realized that I had learned very little in my three years of legal education. Ed Boyko came up with something I had never heard of, a principle called "the best interests of the child." To Boyko it mattered naught that there had been a "mistake" in the doctor's affidavit; what mattered was that the infant child now had a good home with loving parents. According to Boyko, I was "Victorian" in my beliefs in the importance of marriage, I was "tinged with purple" in my moral philosophy, and I was "puerile" in my arguments.

Boyko objected to every one of my attempts to enter evidence into the court record, while he got in every bit of evidence he wanted. In fact, Boyko got in a bunch of stuff that wasn't evidence at all! I was so in awe of what I was observing that I failed to make proper objections. In my naivete, I never considered my opponent, one of the state's best and most knowledgeable attorneys, would try to pull some fast ones on me. If Boyko said something was admissible, no doubt it was. If Boyko said something was not admissible, no doubt it wasn't. My opponent had so much experience and talent that I was in awe of him.

Although I did my best, it was like Tom Thumb versus The Incredible Hulk. After losing the case big-time, I came back to my office after the four- or five-day hearing, feeling more like a punching bag than like an attorney. I realized I had learned more in that hearing about what it means to practice law than I had learned in three years in law school.

But somehow, my loss had long-term benefits. Edgar Boyko liked me because I hadn't quit and just kept fighting. When I got into private practice, years later, Boyko would send me referrals. And when Ed became too elderly and ill to handle his own affairs, he hired me to be his own personal attorney. I always considered that a very high compliment.

Judge Butcher also liked me and he showed it less than a year later.

Chapter 20

Bad News

I worked for the Alaska Department of Law for a year. My title was Assistant Attorney General. But I could hold that title, and practice in Alaskan courts, only until I took the Alaska bar exam and the results came in. If I passed the bar exam, I would be admitted to the Alaska bar and could continue as an assistant AG. If I flunked ... I'd probably have to really take a job selling shoes!

I hadn't had to pass a bar exam to get admitted in Wisconsin. Wisconsin had what was known as "the diploma privilege." Wisconsin had decided that if you graduated from one of the two Wisconsin law schools, you had certainly taken your share of tests in school and one more, a bar exam, was overkill. Our Wisconsin law school diplomas were enough to cause the State of Wisconsin to grant us the privilege of a license to practice law in that state.

But I didn't want to practice law in Wisconsin. I wanted to practice law in Alaska! And Alaska didn't have the diploma privilege. In fact, Alaska didn't even have a law school! To be admitted to the Alaska bar, you had to pass a bar exam, which was given twice a year, in the summer, and in the winter. I arrived in Alaska too late to sign up for the summer 1968 exam so I signed up for the winter 1968-69 exam. I rented a bar review course and began studying in the fall of 1968. I remember many late evenings and long weekends reading each of the basic areas of the law such as contracts, torts, criminal law, constitutional law, evidence, and about another ten or so topics. I also had to study Alaska law, a subject that was not even mentioned at Marquette, much less taught. Of course since Alaska had been admitted as a state only nine years earlier, I arguably had it easier than present-day bar applicants. I only had less than ten years of Alaska Supreme Court decisions to become familiar with. Current applicants have more than fifty years of decisions to study.

The bar exam lasted three days. And then I had to wait several months for the results.

One Friday evening I got a phone call from Western Union advising me that I had been sent a telegram. Hoping that no one in my family had died, I asked the caller to read the telegram to me. It started something like this "The Alaska Bar Association regrets to inform you … " I had flunked the bar exam!

For a fee of $150 I got to sit down with one of the bar exam graders to go over my exam. The grader I met with was Herr Dr. Earnest Rehbock. Herr Dr. Rehbock was so German that he hissed when he spoke. Even with my high school German language lessons, I had trouble under-standing him. He looked like an old European schoolmaster and was a formidable figure but contrary to appearances, he turned out to be a really amiable fellow. He told me I missed passing the bar by only a point or two. He and a fellow named Edward J. Reasor had each given me a passing grade but a lawyer by the name of Sheila Gallagher-no relation to Russ Gallagher mentioned earlier-had given me a less than passing score.

I needed a score of seventy. The scores I got from Dr. Rehbock and Ed Reasor, more than seventy from each, were not enough to overcome the score below seventy that I got from Ms. Gallagher. I wasn't much comforted by the fact that I was one of 64 percent of the applicants who failed the bar that year. Unfortunately, with a 64 percent failure rate, a number of other fellows in the AG's office also failed to pass the bar. Attorney General Edwards now had a majority of his Assistant AGs who could no longer go to court. As a result, he needed to shift personnel. He wanted to send some of us to Juneau and transfer some Juneau folks to Anchorage to man the Anchorage office. Since I lacked any seniority in the Anchorage office, I was asked to go to Juneau. I spoke to Barbara about moving. "We would have gone anywhere when you were first given the job at the AG's," Barbara said "but you were given an Anchorage position. We have now settled here, and I'd vote to stay here"! So I turned down AG Edwards's offer, gave my notice, and began to look for other employment.

I was quickly offered a job by Ed Reasor and took it, starting work with him immediately as a law clerk, and I made preparations for taking the bar exam again[14].

Several weeks later Reasor told me about a position with the Family Court. The judge who was in charge of the Family Court was Harold J. Butcher, who had presided over my first court case in which I had unsuccessfully opposed Edgar Paul Boyko. Reasor had spoken to Judge Butcher about me and the judge suggested to Reasor that I apply for the position. So I did.

I didn't know it then but Reasor's suggestion to me was only one of the many times he was to have a major effect on my career.

---

[14] I passed the bar exam the next time I took it and was admitted to the Alaska Bar in November 1969. I was told that I was the 232nd attorney in Alaska at that time.

Chapter 21
The Family Court

Within a week of submitting my application, I was appointed Standing Master of the Family Court and Court Trustee. My salary was now in excess of $2,000 a month, twice what I had been paid as an assistant attorney general!

In Alaska and some other jurisdictions, a Master is somewhat like a junior judge. Some states call them hearing officers or court commissioners. As a family court master, I presided over various hearings involving children who were neglected or abused (Children in Need of Aid), children who were runaways or truants (Children in Need of Supervision), and children who committed offenses which, if they had been adults, would be considered crimes (Delinquent Children). I also heard uncontested divorce matters.

I had limited authority to issue court orders. Generally, I merely made written recommendations to Judge Butcher on how cases should be disposed of, and Judge Butcher either accepted my recommendations and signed appropriate orders, or overruled me. Most of the time my recommendations were upheld.

After I got the job, I wrote Marquette's assistant dean, Charles Mentkowski, about my new job. "Chuck" Mentkowski had taught me family law in law school and had given me a grade of only 77. In my letter, I told Chuck if the State of Alaska had recognized my talents in family law enough to make me a master of the family court, he obviously had been mistaken in giving me such a mediocre grade in his class. With my tongue clenched firmly in my cheek, I told Chuck that in view of my new appointment I was demanding he raise my grade, *nunc pro tunc* (now as if then).

The author as a Family Court Master (1969-1973).

Chuck wrote back with immediate congratulations, He concluded his letter with the statement: "If you can get such a good job getting only a 77 in my class, think how good a job you could have gotten if you had studied! Request denied!"

Superior Court judges in the Third Judicial District at Anchorage, Alaska in the early 1970s. (Back row, left to right) Judges James Singleton, Harold Butcher, Ed Burke, James Hanson, and Connie Occhipinti - (Front row, left to right) Judges Ralph Moody, Edward Davis, James Fitzgerald, and Eben Lewis.

———

As court trustee, I had the responsibility of collecting child support from divorced parents who did not have custody of their children, but who had the responsibility of paying it to the parents who did have custody. During the period I held that office, we installed and implemented a computerized system which told us who failed to make child support payments, who was behind in their payments, and who had paid as they had been ordered to do. The computerized system also prepared monthly billings, which we mailed to those persons ordered to pay.

———

Those were the days when the best piece of office equipment for typing letters was the electric typewriter. Whenever I wanted to send a letter, I liked to call a secretary in and dictate the letter to her. She'd write down my dictation using shorthand, and then go type my letter.

Since there weren't a lot of secretaries who knew shorthand, however, often I would either have to write my letters out, longhand, or dictate them on a machine called a Dictaphone. The Dictaphone had a circular belt that would record my dictation. Later it had a recording tape. The secretary took the belt, or the tape, and put it into her machine, which she operated with a foot pedal. She'd hit the foot pedal, the tape played into her earphones, and she typed up what she heard, hitting the foot pedal to stop the tape until she could catch up to the dictation. Then with her foot pedal, she'd advance the belt or tape a bit more, and type that up.

One secretary I had for a while was a terrible speller. I always got my letters back from her with a few words misspelled. I'd circle the misspelled words, and ask her to retype the letter. When I got the letter back the second time, she'd have the first errors corrected, but then misspell other words even though she had spelled them right on the first draft.

After a while, in an effort to get her to proofread what she had typed, I'd cease circling the misspelled words. Instead, I'd simply send her letter back to her with a note saying she had misspelled three words, or four words, without saying which words were misspelled. I wanted her to locate them herself and then correct them.

Finally I noticed that when I pointed out she had misspelled a specific number of words, I did not get a corrected letter back from her for several days. Apparently she was hoping I would forget the number of errors she had made on the first draft, and she'd simply submit the first draft back to me a second time.

That game was one I was unwilling to play very long. I finally had to let her go.

———

Whenever someone fell behind in his child support, or failed to make any payments at all, we'd first send them a nice letter suggesting they bring their payments current. If that letter did not achieve the desired result, we'd set up a hearing and have the judge issue an order to show cause directing the recalcitrant payor to appear in court on a certain day to show cause "if any he has" why he should not be found in contempt for not making the court-ordered payments.

Often these contempt hearings were held before the presiding judge, Ralph E. Moody. Moody was a curmudgeon and I liked to have my contempt hearings scheduled before him. He didn't waste much time. The payor appeared in front of Moody. Moody asked the payor if he had failed to make the payment. Generally the payor admitted that he had, indeed, failed to make the required payment and then attempted to explain why the payment had been missed. Moody always interrupted the payor, and told him there would be a hearing the next day at which the payor would have the opportunity to make his excuses. Moody then set the time of the hearing, and advised the payor the following: "If you bring your payments current by tomorrow, you need not appear and Mr. Ross can cancel the hearing. If your payments aren't current by tomorrow, you can tell me why they are not current and I'll consider what you have to say. My suggestion is, however, that if your payments are not current by tomorrow, you had better bring your toothbrush with you … because you may not be going home for a while."

Moody's admonishment worked wonders. Overnight most delinquent payors were able to find money where earlier they had assured me that no money existed!

Sometimes the payor ignored the order to show cause and simply failed to appear in court at the time specified. Then my office issued a warrant for that person's arrest and the troopers or the city police sought him out and brought him before the court.

On occasion a recalcitrant payor was hard to find. That's when I'd call for Alaska State Trooper Gene Rudolph. I called him "Bulldog Rudolph." Bulldog could track a raindrop into next week. If Bulldog was on your trail, the only way you could escape him was to die before you were caught.

Bulldog Rudolph made two arrests that I can remember to this day. On one occasion he arrested a guy at the guy's father's funeral. "I took him away in handcuffs, right beside the coffin!" Bulldog explained. "Of course I let him pay his respects first. Then I told him he was under arrest!"

Nobody could ever say Bulldog didn't have a heart.

On another occasion, Bulldog arrested a groom in the back of a church, just after the groom had walked down the aisle with his just-married new bride. "The bride kept yelling at me," Bulldog said later. "She wanted to know why I was arresting her new husband. When I told her the warrant was for failure to pay child support, she started yelling at her new husband. Apparently he had never told her that he was the father of any kids! I'm not sure that marriage will last," Bulldog surmised.

———

Once a guy was arrested, he was brought into court as soon as possible. In such cases, Moody again continued the matter for a day and give the payor the toothbrush admonishment. Sometimes he released the fellow until the next day; sometimes he'd let him languish overnight in jail. Either way, the arrearage was usually paid within twenty-four hours. It was a great system, and it worked.

One fellow, a guide named Lloyd, lived just south of Glennallen, a town about 185 miles northeast of Anchorage. Lloyd was always late in his payments and sometimes failed to appear for a "show cause" hearing. I'd then get a warrant out for him and he'd be arrested and the troopers would haul him into town. Once Lloyd got to town he'd pay his child support arrearage. I asked him once why he didn't just pay on time and avoid being arrested. "When I get arrested, I get a free ride to town!" Lloyd explained. "I save money that way!"

We eventually developed a good system and got the attention of payors. Deadbeats got to know that if they didn't pay we'd be on them like stink on a skunk. Our collection of child support became quite successful.

Then someone had to spoil the process. A guy named Johansson failed to pay his child support and appealed our method of operation to the Alaska Supreme Court. The Supreme Court held that a payor who claimed inability to pay had a right to a jury trial. Thus, if a fellow *refused* to pay his child support a judge could put him in jail in order to compel him to pay. And that fellow could remain in jail until he did pay. On the other hand, the Supreme Court held, a payor who *claimed inability* to pay could not be simply incarcerated summarily. Instead, a jury would have to be empaneled if he so requested, and it would be the jury's duty to decide the question of whether the payor could or could not have paid.

Of course, once the Johansson decision was released, nobody ever refused to pay; instead, they all alleged that they simply could not afford to pay. Jury trials were long and costly and the system began to bog down. There were a lot of mothers and kids who did not receive child support because we could not provide jury trials to everyone who demanded one. Eventually the legislature enacted laws which authorized other procedures, besides incarceration, to facilitate child support enforcement.

———

Most of the uncontested divorces I heard were pretty dull. A few, though, I remember well.

In one case, a woman appeared who claimed she wanted a divorce because of her husband's cruelty. When I asked her what it was that her husband had done that was cruel, she testified that he had slammed her hand in a car door, breaking her finger. Noticing that none of her fingers bore a bandage, I asked her when the car door incident had occurred.

"Twenty-seven years ago!" she replied.

Quite obviously elephants are not the only ones with a long memory.

Another case involved a Polish girl who testified that her marriage to her husband had been arranged by her parents while she lived in Poland. The man they picked for their daughter to marry was at least forty years older than she was but, according to her parents, he was from America and would take his new wife there. The bride met her groom for the first time on the day of the marriage. True to his promise, the groom brought his bride to America where, according to the girl, she was kept in virtual bondage. She related that she had to wait on her husband hand and foot and that he often brought friends to the house and expected her to wait on them also. She also testified that her husband was brutal and abusive and that she was often beaten by him. She stated that her husband had threatened to kill her if she ever tried to leave him.

As this lady was testifying, I noticed that her husband, who was sitting across the hearing table from her, was becoming more and more angry. He was a little, balding man, and looked like the movie stereotype of a KGB agent. He had a suit coat on and his right hand was slowly edging into a position where it appeared he intended to draw a gun from a shoulder holster under his coat. At the time I had taken to carrying a Smith & Wesson Model 60 .38 special revolver, with a Hip-Grip, under my robes. I slowly slipped my hand through the pocket of my black robe and pulled the revolver out under the table. By this time, the man's right hand had disappeared into his coat under his left arm.

"Mr. _____!" I told him. "I want both your hands on the table immediately!"

The man glared at me and slowly moved his hand from under his coat. I fully expected a gun to appear in his hand but he eventually put both his empty hands on the table. "Keep both your hands where I can see them!" I ordered. And he did.

When the hearing finished I told the fellow to remain in the hearing room until his now ex-wife and her attorney, Bill Erwin, left the room. I then allowed the man to leave. Two or three minutes later one of the court clerks rushed into the room. "Judge Ross!" she said. "Have you had the _____ vs. _____ case yet?"

I told her that the hearing had just ended.

"I hurried here as fast as I could! I wanted to warn you!" she exclaimed. "We just got a call telling us that Mr. _____ has a .45 pistol under his coat and he has been telling people he was going down to the courthouse to shoot his wife!"

I thanked her for the warning which, of course, came a bit late. But something had warned me that the man was very dangerous and I had been fully prepared had that been necessary. I am glad nothing happened, however. The hearing room was very small and things could have gone south very fast.

Nowadays the judges have little alarm buttons they can push, the courtrooms are monitored via video, and metal detectors are staffed at the courthouse entrances. Not so in those days.

———

The family court had a juvenile intake officer whose job it was to determine which kids who got into trouble could be handled on an informal basis and which kids needed to be brought before the court on delinquency charges. Jay Warner was a hard-working, energetic fellow who really enjoyed his job. He was good at putting the fear of God into kids before handling their cases with informal probation. And he was good at knowing which kids needed more than a talking-to. Those were the kids Jay would file charges against and those were the kids who appeared in my court.

Jay and I were in court together one day. I forget now what kind of matter it was but there was an older Alaska Native woman whom I could not understand. She had a big "hocker" of tobacco she was chewing on and, as a result, she was slurring her words. Finally, in order to understand her, I needed to have her get rid of her snoose. Wanting to be polite, I said to her, "Ma'am, would you please remove your gum, so that I can understand you?"

She looked at me and said "What do you want me to do with it?"

Jay Warner had not noticed that the lady was chewing tobacco so he put his hand out, offering to throw her "gum" away for her. Only it wasn't gum.

Looking at Jay's hand, the lady wiped a finger through her mouth, came out with her wad of snoose, and dumped it into Jay's outstretched palm. Jay looked at it for a second, looked at me, and realized that I had known what the lady had been chewing. He got up, walked around the hearing room, gingerly carrying the handful of tobacco, and slid behind my chair to reach the wastebasket. Somehow, he kicked the wheels on my chair and I went over backwards onto the floor. Jay claimed it was an accident and apologized profusely, of course. But I doubted his sincerity. My being dumped was simply too timely. My courtroom really lacked decorum that day.

———

Some cases the family court considered involved kids who were what we called "incorrigible." They would not abide by curfews, skipped school, didn't obey their parents, or even ran away. They were called Children in Need of Supervision, or CHINS.

When a CHINS kid came to the attention of the court, Jay Warner might try informal probation in an attempt to get the kid to abide by the rules at home or school. If the kid still didn't behave, Warner filed a CHINS petition with the court. When such a petition was filed, the kid and his parents appeared in court and if the kid admitted the charge, or if after a trial the petition had been proven, I had to decide what to do about the problem.

If the matter was fairly serious, I'd place the child in lockup at the McLaughlin Youth Center (MYC) and schedule a disposition hearing several weeks later. At the disposition hearing, after enduring several weeks at MYC the kid was usually willing to go home and behave himself.

Seldom did we have to lock a child up at MYC very long. Locking up a child at MYC was "reality therapy" and worked quite well. The kid realized things were a lot better at home than they were at MYC.

Unfortunately, somebody appealed the issue of whether or not a CHINS could be locked up. Their theory was if a kid didn't want to stay home and abide by the rules, it must be the parents' fault.

Once again the Alaska Supreme Court mucked things up. It decided no kid could be locked up unless he or she had committed a delinquent act, that is, unless the kid had committed an act which if he had been an adult, could have been prosecuted as a crime.

The appealed case involved a girl who continuously ran away. One professional described her as having "the rabbit complex." She could not, or would not, stay in one place.

On one occasion, she fled to California with an older adult male and supported herself, and him, through acts of prostitution. Since the prostitution occurred in California, she could not be prosecuted in Alaska.

Her parents were at their wits' end, and realistically feared for the girl's safety. I had her locked up in MYC and Judge Butcher sustained my decision. The Supreme Court, however, ordered her freed.

Nonetheless, we delayed freeing the girl until we could find a suitable placement. Finally, we were able to place her in one of the state's finest foster homes. Two days later, the girl ran from that foster home, just as she had run away from her parents. To my knowledge, no one ever saw her again. I often wonder what happened to her.

Another such case involved a boy who continuously skipped school and refused to obey his parents. The parents described him as "a ticking time bomb" and feared he would cause serious harm if he was not locked up.

After the Supreme Court decision that we could no longer incarcerate CHINS, we could not lock up the boy, even temporarily. We tried foster placement, which didn't work any more than placement at home. Eventually, as predicted by his parents, the boy set a church on fire causing many tens of thousands of dollars of damages. The arson was, of course, a delinquent act, so we could finally lock him up. It was a bit late, however, because the church was a total loss.

———

Judge Butcher and I both testified in front of the Legislature with suggestions as to changes which should be made to the Children's Rules. Representative Genie Chance chaired the legislative committee, if I recall, and our proposed changes went nowhere. The do-gooders in the legislature were all too often willing to blame the parents for a kid's bad behavior. I believed then, and still believe, that despite some parents' best efforts, there are a lot of outside influences at school and in the community that can cause a kid to go wrong. It isn't always the parents' fault.

One case did demonstrate parental fault, however, and I remember it quite well. A boy had been brought before me for stealing tires. After the kid admitted the charges, I had to decide what to do about the matter. The boy and his parents wanted him to go home.

"How do I know you aren't going to steal again?" I asked the boy.

His dad answered for him. "He won't steal again!" his dad promised. "Our son stole the tires to sell so he could buy a motorcycle. We are going to buy him that motorcycle! That way he won't have any reason to steal again!"

I sentenced the boy to a term at MYC. If I could have, I would have sentenced his folks to be locked up too!

Later, the boy-by then an adult-reportedly killed the family of a well-known Alaskan. Several months later, the boy himself was found murdered near Potter's Marsh, allegedly as a payback for killing that family. I

The author and Judge Harold Butcher at the National Juvenile Court
Judges Association meeting in Milwaukee, Wisconsin (circa 1972).

don't think either crime was officially solved. Certainly, nobody was prosecuted. But I understand everybody in law enforcement knows who did
what, and why.

———

Judge Butcher and I became members of the National Juvenile Court
Judges Association (NJCJA). One year the NJCJA had its annual meeting
in Milwaukee. Knowing that I was from Milwaukee, Judge Butcher invited
me to go to those meetings with him. We had a great time and I enjoyed
showing him my hometown.

At one of the sessions, Judge Butcher stood up to speak and the moderator ruled him out of order. Judge Butcher was quite angry. I stood up and appealed the decision of the chair. I said we had come almost 4000 miles and that the judge deserved the opportunity to be heard. A vote to sustain the chair was taken, and the chair was not sustained. As a result Judge Butcher got to speak. He later asked me "Where did you learn that trick?"

I didn't tell him that parliamentary procedure was one of only two courses I had gotten an A in at Marquette. Sometimes it is better to leave a person guessing.

Chapter 22
My First Moose

After living in Alaska for one year, I officially became a resident, allowing me to purchase a resident hunting license. As a resident, I did not have to purchase game tags for animals I chose to hunt. Game tags are expensive and a nonresident must purchase a separate one for each species of game hunted. To a resident, however, game tags were free.

In those days there were two seasons for moose, an early season in September and a late season in November. A day or two before the end of the second season, Barb and I had been invited to Chet and Virginia Paulk's house for dinner. I was introduced to Chet and Virginia's son-in-law and his twin brother. The Wielers, Paul and Scott, were big gregarious guys, each one weighing around 300 pounds or more. I took to calling them "the Tons of Fun."

After dinner we got to talking about hunting. I told them I planned on going moose hunting to the Petersville mine road the last day of the season. I invited them along. I figured guys their size would be useful if I had to pack a moose out of the woods for any distance. David Pree, my former employer's son, was going to go also. David was more than 200 pounds himself.

The plan was to leave early and meet Steve Dunning, an assistant district attorney, at the Forks Roadhouse, which is situated about Mile 19 of the Petersville Mine Road. Dunning had planned to go in several days earlier to "look over the area." "If there is a moose in the area, I'll know about it!" Steve promised. "You guys meet me at the Forks between 8 and 8:30 Sunday morning and then we'll go after it!"

Sunday morning, 8 AM, found me, David, and the Tons of Fun, in my Chevelle station wagon, driving the Petersville mine road towards the Forks. A fresh snow was falling and there were four or five inches on the ground already. Several miles before the roadhouse, we saw fresh tracks going across the road. We stopped and checked them out. Moose tracks! Less than a hundred yards down the road was another set of moose tracks.

My companions wanted to stop and follow the tracks but I had promised Steve Dunning that I would meet him and so we pressed on.

We got to the Forks at 8:35 AM, only to find Dunning gone. "He waited until 8:30," the lodge owner stated, "and then he took off! Said he was going hunting."

I was a bit disappointed in Steve. He could see it was snowing and he could and should have given us a little extra time before leaving the Forks. So rather than chasing after Steve we decided to go back to the moose tracks we had seen, and follow them.

We parked the car between the two sets of tracks, loaded up, and headed into the woods. We hadn't gone more than twenty feet when one of the Wielers whispered, "There's a moose!"

I whispered back, "There's two of them! You take the one on the left and I'll take the one on the right!"

We both shot at about the same time and two moose fell dead. We had legally taken a cow and a yearling bull!

I hadn't realized how big moose are in comparison to the whitetails of Wisconsin I had been used to packing. But now the Tons of Fun came in very handy. They both knew how to cut up the moose and they both were great packers. Not that we had to pack very far. Both moose had fallen within seventy-five yards of my car.

We put down the back seat and loaded two moose into the back of the wagon. We put me and the Tons of Fun in the front seat and David had to crawl into the back on top of the moose meat. The rear bumper of my car was only two or three inches off the ground and the headlights, when we finally had to turn them on, were pointed up into the night sky.

We drove back to the Forks Roadhouse and parked outside. When we walked in, there was Steve Dunning, having a cup of coffee. "Sorry we missed you Steve!" I stated. "How'd you do?"

Steve said he hadn't seen a thing in three days. "There's no sign of moose around here!" he muttered.

I invited Steve to come outside. "We saw a couple," I told him. "Too bad you didn't wait for us!" My hunting companions and I then got in the Chevelle and drove off, leaving Steve outside the roadhouse clutching his cup of coffee.

It was a slow ride home. I worried the whole way about breaking a spring or two on my car.

The next night we all went to Chet Paulk's garage. The Tons of Fun knew how to butcher a moose, also, and they willingly showed me how it was done.

Chapter 23
Macie's Gun

I have always liked large-caliber firearms. Some (friends) say it's because I am a high-caliber person myself. Others (more numerous) think it is because I am somewhat of a big bore. Whatever the reason, I like large-caliber firearms.

The first time I saw Macie's .458, I knew I'd have to own it. That was even before I knew its history.

I was visiting Macie's widow. Luigi was a young gal in her fifties and we were discussing her recently deceased husband and his interest, like mine, in firearms. Would I like to see his guns, she asked?

Would I? Is the Pope Catholic?

After showing me a Navy Luger and a Giles 45, both of which I later acquired, Luigi brought out the .458. It was beautiful. It was an early FN action with a jeweled bolt, mounted on a custom Monte Carlo stock, with a custom barrel having a Cutts Compensator on the end. Luigi explained she carried the .458 as a backup bear gun while moose hunting with her .300 Magnum. She stated the .458 kicked a bit so she had the Cutts Compensator put on as a muzzle brake to control some of the recoil. She said the first time she fired it, she made the mistake of shooting it under a tin roof at a firing range. The Cutts deflected the muzzle blast upward, hitting the tin roof and she was deaf for a week.

I tried to buy the rifle. It wasn't for sale. I did wrestle a promise from Luigi that if she ever did decide to sell it, I'd get first crack at it.

That evening, I read up on the .458. The .458 Winchester Magnum cartridge shoots a 510-grain soft-point bullet of almost .46 caliber at a muzzle velocity of 2,110 feet per second with a muzzle energy of 5,041 foot-pounds. For comparison, the .30-06 shoots a 220-grain .30-caliber bullet at a muzzle velocity of 2,410 feet per second with a muzzle energy of 2,837 foot-pounds. The .458 has close to twice the power of a .30-06 and is used extensively in Africa on such things as elephants.

From that time on, I saw several other .458s. None impressed me as much as Macie's, with its clean, smooth lines.

I kept in touch with Luigi during the ensuing years and often sought to buy the .458 but it was "not for sale." Then one evening Luigi called. She had just come from her doctor. The news was not good. It appeared that her health prevented her from any further hunting. Was I still interested in buying the .458? If so, I was to take it to several gun shops, get it appraised, and make her an offer.

I picked up the .458 and, after getting its value from two shops, I visited the third, Mountain View Sports Center.

Upon viewing the rifle, Jack Shine, then the gunsmith at Mountain View Sports Center, looked at me suspiciously. "Where did you get Macie's gun?" he asked.

After explaining the circumstances to him, Shine said, "I'm the guy who put this new stock on, after the bear chewed up the old one." When I inquired further, Shine did not respond directly. Holding the rifle up to his shoulder, then taking it down and turning it over in his hands, he eventually said, "This rifle saved Macie's life and killed him." Shine then proceeded to tell me the story of that rifle.

Macie had the rifle custom-built by Shine. He then took the rifle to Kodiak for a bear hunt. Apparently Macie or someone else in his party wounded a large brown bear with the rifle. The bear disappeared into a patch of alders. Then, before Macie could fire a second shot the bear was on him. Macie shoved the rifle sideways at the bear's mouth as the bear tried to bite his leg. The bear bit into the rifle instead of the leg and ran a few steps past Macie with the rifle. In those fleeting seconds Macie debated whether or not to try shooting the bear with the .44 Magnum revolver he had in a shoulder holster. He decided against it. If the big .458 hadn't killed the bear when he'd shot it the first time, a .44 magnum might only infuriate the bear further. In less time than it takes to tell the story, the bear dropped the rifle and reentered the alders. Macie went to the .458, and, as Shine told it, "wiped the slobber off." Raising the rifle Macie caught sight of the bear's head in the alders and shot again, killing the bear.

"Y'know," said Shine, "Macie felt poorly after that. Even got sick to his stomach." Upon his return to Anchorage, Macie brought the gun back to Shine. The stock had teeth marks all over it. The blueing was even marred by the bear's teeth. Shine reblued the rifle and replaced the stock.

Macie continued to feel ill and eventually went to see a doctor. "You've suffered a heart attack," he was told. The only thing Macie could figure out was he suffered the heart attack when the bear came at him out of the alders.

"Macie had never had any heart problems before the incident" said Shine. "A year later he died of heart trouble. That's why I say this rifle saved his life and killed him."

Upon my return to Luigi's home, I asked her if the rifle had any interesting history behind it. She then related essentially the same story.

I bought the rifle.

For several years Luigi tried to get me the bear hide and tooth-marked stock. Macie's relatives, however, have the hide and stock hanging in their bar in Northern Michigan and have refused to part with them.

Would I like to have that tooth-marked stock? Is the Pope Catholic?

———

Simpson Bay is about ten minutes flying time north of Cordova, Alaska. There's a Forest Service cabin there that is available for rental for a few days at a time. There's also a great abundance of bears at Simpson Bay. I know.

In 1972, Bob Rink, a friend of mine who's an above-average real estate broker, and I decided to try to do some goose and deer hunting in and around Prince William Sound.

We checked with the Forest Service in Cordova. While at the Forest Service office there, Alaska State Trooper Ron Cole stopped in. We got to talking, and he advised us to try Simpson Bay where, he said, there was a good supply of deer and geese.

"Take a big gun along though," Ron advised. "There are a lot of bears over there."

Bob Rink and I departed the next morning for Simpson Bay. Bob had my .30-06 and a shotgun, and I took a Browning semiautomatic 12-gauge and Macie's .458. We also each had a .45-caliber revolver and hoped to get a deer with them.

We had rented the Forest Service cabin at Simpson Bay. The first night after dinner, we went out from the cabin toward a small stream to fill up our water bottles. On the way we had something very big follow along beside us in the woods, keeping just out of the light of the lantern. From the sounds of the trees being knocked down, we were sure it was a big bear. Elephants aren't indigenous to Prince William Sound.

The next day we hunted geese and deer, without success. About 4 p.m. we returned to the cabin. Bob decided to take a nap while I hiked up to a small lake behind the cabin. I grabbed the Browning 12-gauge, figuring that I might get a shot at a goose up at the lake, but then remembering the incident of the night before, and Trooper Cole's warning about bears, I changed my mind and took the .458.

The trail to Milton Lake meandered along a small stream, crossing back and forth over bridges made from single logs. Salmon still splashed in the stream although the run was coming to a close. As I skirted old salmon bones along the path, I remember thinking I was glad it was October and not during the peak salmon run because it was clear that many bears had been in the area during the peak of the spawning.

About halfway to the lake the trail led around some bushes, taking me out of sight of the stream for a few moments. At that time I heard a substantial amount of splashing ahead and to my left. I thought it sounded as if there might have been some barrier across the stream, causing the salmon to school below the obstruction. I came around the bushes, and the stream returned to view but it wasn't salmon causing the splashing.

Instead, three bears were in front of me. One bear was sixty feet away looking at me. The second bear was fifty feet away, also looking at me. The third bear was forty feet away and coming right at me. Instinctively I raised my rifle.

As the gun came up I can recall three distinct thoughts. The first was, "This can't be happening to me! This only happens in *Field and Stream* magazine!" The second thought was, "There are three bears and you have only three cartridges in this rifle!" And the third thought was a remembrance of a picture hanging in a friend's office. It's a Charles Russell print of a cowboy who had been leading some horses along the rim of an arroyo. The horses are bucking. One bear is dead at the cowboy's feet. The second has ahold of his boot as the cowboy fires his Winchester at the bear, and the third bear is still coming.

Those three thoughts raced through my mind in far less time than it takes to tell. The .458 went off. I never felt the recoil. All I knew was one minute the bear was coming at me full tilt; the next, the bear had cartwheeled over backwards just as if it had run full speed into a brick wall. It never moved.

I thought the noise of the gun would scare the other two bears off. I chambered another round. The other two bears didn't flinch at the sound. One bear started walking towards the side like he intended to try and get around behind me. The other bear started walking towards me. "Ross," I said to myself. "What's a nice Milwaukee boy like you doing in a place like this? Get the hell out of here!"

I started backing up, keeping my eye and the rifle on the bear coming toward me while still trying to watch the one trying to flank me, and still trying to watch the one I had hit to make sure it didn't get up again. As I backed up, the bear coming towards me matched me step for step, keeping about 50 feet away. I finally came to one of the log bridges, hot-footed it across, and beat a hasty retreat back to the cabin.

By that time, the plane had come in to deposit the third member of our group, Dr. Curtis Menard Sr., dentist of Wasilla.

"What happened to you?" he said. "You're white as a sheet."

"I just had to shoot a brownie," I told him.

"Why, you can't do that!" he said. "Brown bear season doesn't open for another week."

"Well," I said, "human season isn't open either and this bear was about to violate."

We discussed the matter and my friends pointed out that the Fish and Game Department required that a person shooting a bear in defense of life or property salvage the hide and skull. Rink and Menard were all in favor of heading back up the trail to skin out my bear.

"Listen," I said. "He's got two big friends with him up there, and they're both pissed at me. Besides, it's getting dark. And I'm not going back up there tonight with two more bears up there."

I don't think that at the time Rink and Menard believed me about three bears, but they agreed that we'd wait until morning.

Early the next day, we hiked back up the trail to skin out my bear. Menard had a .44-magnum revolver, and Rink had a .45 revolver and the Browning automatic 12-gauge, plug removed, loaded alternatively with double 00 buck and slugs. I had a .45 and the .458.

I had read somewhere that in bear country a person should carry a bell or a tin can full of stones to warn the bears away. Don't believe it. The Good Humor man has a bell on his truck and it certainly doesn't scare the kids away. I think bears hear a noise like that and think it's a dinner bell, and I'll tell you why I think so.

We didn't have a bell or cans with stones so we took some pots and pans and banged them together as we walked up the trail. We also sang bawdy songs, figuring Rink's voice was enough to scare anything away.

When we got to my bear we paced off the distance from the bear to where I shot from. Eleven steps. Too close for comfort.

We then started working on skinning the bear. As I was skinning out one of the paws, I noticed Rink put the shotgun down to assist Menard on the skinning. "What are you doing?" I asked him.

"Helping you skin the bear!" he answered.

"You can help us best by picking up that shotgun and keeping your eyes open. There are still two more bears around here," I told him.

"I'm sure if there were other bears around, we've scared them away with our pots and pans and singing," he replied.

"Bob," I said. "Do me a favor and pick up the shotgun and stand guard!"

Rink complied. He picked up the shotgun, walked up on the bank and started whistling nonchalantly as Menard and I resumed skinning.

Suddenly I heard Rink exclaim "Oh, sugar!" (Now that's not really what he said, but you may want to read this story to your kids, and who am I to poison the minds of children.)

I knew instinctively what Rink meant. "Go for your gun!" I yelled to Menard as I came up with the .458.

Sure enough, here came those other two bears again, running right toward us. Did you know bears can leap more than five-foot logs? I didn't.

Until then.

Now I knew the Alaska Fish and Game Department might believe defense of life for one dead bear. I was more doubtful they would believe it with three dead bears so, as they came at us, we proceeded to insult the bears' parentage no end. We called them every name in the book and then some.

"If they get to that log, we'll have to shoot," I said. Just before the log, about fifty feet away, they stopped and stood up on their hind legs. Both bears were bigger than the one I shot. It would have made a great photograph but I wasn't about to put the .458 down to take a picture.

After more insults being hurled in their direction-I think Rink even sang a song-the bears dropped down on all fours and disappeared back into the woods.

We quickly finished the skinning and got out of there. The plane picked us up and we returned to Cordova.

The author, left, carrying the bear hide, and Dr. Curtis Menard,
right, at Simpson Bay, Alaska (1972).

We turned the hide and skull in to Rod Mills, protection officer with
the Alaska Fish & Game in Cordova.

"How do you know that bear was charging?" Rod Mills asked.

"Well, Rod," I said, "I've thought about that. Perhaps he wasn't. Perhaps
he smelled and heard me coming up the trail and just was trying to get away
and had the misfortune to run in my direction. Perhaps he was even the
Welcome Wagon coming to welcome me to the neighborhood. I guess I
would have never really ascertained his intentions until I allowed him to
take a bite out of my leg. But I wasn't about to let him get that close!"

"Were you wearing that hat?" Rod Mills asked, referring to my large
Elmer-Keith-style Australian Akubra version of a Montana cowboy hat.

I replied that I had indeed been wearing my hat when charged.

"That bear probably saw your hat and your beard and figured you
were the south end of another bear going north," Rod Mills explained.

The more I think about it, the more I'm convinced I was being insulted.

Chapter 24
Running with Judge Butcher

While I was working at the family court, Barbara and I lived about a mile from the courthouse and I used to walk to work on nice days. Judge Butcher lived about a mile farther from the courthouse than I did.

When the judge heard I was walking to and from work, he told me that he "ran" home every night and asked me if I'd like to "run" with him. At that time I was a young man of twenty-eight or twenty-nine and the judge was in his mid sixties.

"Sure, I'll run with you!" I answered, never realizing the ordeal that was in store for me. After all, when a guy more than sixty-five claims that he runs home, he couldn't really mean that he runs home, could he?

I met the judge in his chambers after work. He had a jogging suit on. That should have been my first warning, but it wasn't. "Are you ready?" he asked.

"Sure!" I said, full of confidence.

I figured the judge and I would jog a bit, and then settle down into a fast walk. It didn't work that way.

When we got outside the courthouse, the judge started out running! And I mean he was running! I hurried after.

I figured he'd slow down after the first block.

He didn't.

He didn't slow down after the second block either.

By the third block, I was getting worried. The judge looked at me as we ran down the sidewalk and said, "You'll get your second wind soon." Unfortunately, I hadn't even gotten my first wind yet!

By the fifth block I was starting to pray we would come across some stop lights that were against us so we'd have to slow down. We didn't. We kept running!

I kept up with him, but only barely, determined that I would continue to do so or die in the attempt.

By the time we had gone about a mile, I was really puffing. The judge wasn't even sweating. "Here's where I turn off," I said to the judge.

"OK!" he said. "See you tomorrow!" and he went running off down the street. I kept up the pace until a school hid me from his view, and then I almost collapsed. I hobbled the rest of the way home.

When Barb answered the door, she asked, "What happened to you? You look like you are about to have a heart attack!"

"An old man just ran the pants off me!" I answered. "And if I do have a heart attack, I hope it's fatal. I couldn't stand the embarrassment of living after being beaten in a footrace by a guy forty years older than I am!"

The next day the judge asked if I wanted to run home with him again. I told him I had an important engagement right after work. I made sure I had important engagements after work every day thereafter.

Several years later, when I opened my own law office, the judge had retired. I asked him to come work with me in my office but he said he wanted to enjoy his retirement, and didn't want to work anymore. I know we would have had fun if he had come to work with me.

After the judge went to the Pioneer Home, I would go see him from time to time. I always visited on Father's Day. He had been as good to me as my own father was, although in a different way.

One Father's Day, I visited the judge when his family was visiting. They were having difficulty getting him to respond to them, and so was I. Then I started telling the story of how the judge ran me into the ground. He seemed to be listening intently, and pretty soon he was laughing along with the rest. He remembered that story and knew what I was talking about.

Judge Harold Butcher died in 1992 at the age of 86. He was a great guy and a good friend.

Chapter 25
Moving On

I enjoyed working with Judge Butcher at the family court. In those days, unlike today, the family court was a separate division of the Anchorage Superior Court. Judge Moody presided over the Anchorage Superior Court and Judge Butcher presided over the family court. There seemed to be an underlying feud between those two courts. I don't know if it was jealousy or some desire for more power but a number of things happened that demonstrated Judge Butcher was in a battle to keep his family court separate from the other judges, and especially from Judge Moody.

On one occasion I heard that the clerk of the superior court, Anna May Vokachek, had prepared a written personnel evaluation on Ginger, one of the young ladies who worked in my office. Anna May recommended Ginger not get a pay increase. Anna May did not know this young lady, and may not even have met her.

I was Ginger's direct supervisor and I was the one who was supposed to do her evaluation. I had already done that evaluation and had recommended Ginger for a much-deserved raise.

Both Judge Butcher and I were a bit incensed that Anna May had submitted a personnel evaluation on one of our employees, and especially a negative one. So I prepared and submitted a written personnel evaluation on one of Anna May's employees.

Anna May was furious. She immediately contacted Judge Butcher and complained to him. She wanted to know what right did I have to evaluate one of her staff? Judge Butcher told her I had as much right to evaluate one of her staff as she had to evaluate one of mine! Anna May backed off and Ginger got her raise.

Every winter Judge Butcher spent a week or two in Hawaii. When he left for Hawaii in 1973, he told me to keep the files locked up and not release them to anyone outside our family court office. A day or two before Judge Butcher was to return, I received a demand for one of our files from Judge Moody. I quickly typed up a written request for Judge Moody's signature and had one of our staff take it to him so that he could sign it, as a court order. I figured with such an order, Judge Butcher would not object to my releasing our file. The next thing I knew, there was a phone call from Judge Moody. "Get your ass up here with that file!" Judge Moody commanded.

I took my proposed order and went to Moody's chambers. "Give me the Goddamn file!" Moody commanded. I explained to the judge that I was just following Judge Butcher's instructions and if Judge Moody would simply sign the order I had prepared, he could have the file. "You're fired!" Judge Moody thundered. "Vacate your office and get out of the courthouse!"

I left Judge Moody's office. I didn't give him the file. Instead, I locked up the file in our file cabinet, secured the key in Judge Butcher's chambers, and left the courthouse. I heard that a few minutes later a state trooper came by my office to make sure I had gone.

That night, Judge Butcher called me at home from Hawaii. He asked me how many employees we had working in the family court. He was getting on a plane back to Anchorage and wanted to make sure he had bought enough pineapples for every employee in the family court.

"Besides yourself, there are twelve people working at the Family Court," I told him.

"There are thirteen!" the Judge insisted.

"Only twelve!" I assured him. "I was fired today!" Then I explained to Judge Butcher what happened. Judge Butcher was very angry. He told me to report back to work the next morning.

The next day I went back to my office. Judge Butcher told me I had followed his instructions and acted properly. The only thing he felt I had done wrong was vacating my office. He said he would rather have had me hauled bodily from my office by the troopers instead of simply leaving the office as I had done.

Judge Butcher had some kind of "come to Jesus" meeting with Judge Moody and the whole thing went away. But as I had when I left my employment with Kohl's food store years earlier, I decided I really didn't like working for someone else and not being my own boss.

I also began to realize by working at the family court, I was picking up a lot of law and experience in a very limited area. There were a lot of other areas of the law I was interested in, and I was not getting any experience in those areas. And finally, I also found myself getting arrogant and I didn't like being that way. If I ever hoped to be able to open my own law office, I still had a lot to learn.

For several months thereafter, I thought about leaving my job at the court system.

———

During my tenure at the court, a lot of great things had happened.

Our first son, Gregory Alexander-McKenzie Ross was born! I was thrilled to be a dad, and still am.

We also purchased a vacant lot at 1326 P Street, several blocks from downtown. Shortly thereafter, we built a duplex on that property. We moved in on New Year's Eve of 1970 with the help of several dear friends.

Barbara, Greg, and I lived in the top unit and we rented out the bottom unit. The rent we received helped make the mortgage payment.

Our duplex was next door to the home of the chief of police, John Flannigan. John was an interesting character. On one occasion he appeared on television in an attempt to recruit police officers. "We are looking for men of the highest moral turpitude!" Chief Flannigan announced. I never heard how successful that recruiting drive was.

On another occasion, on a Saturday afternoon, I received a tip that a deadbeat dad for whom I had issued an arrest warrant was at the Alley Cat Bar. I went next door and asked John to accompany me to arrest the guy.

"Who? Me? The Alley Cat Bar? Not me!" was John's response. "I'm the Chief of Police! I don't arrest anybody!"

I finally was able to get my good friend Barry Ingalls, an Alaska state trooper, to go with me. Barry is about six feet seven inches tall, and when we approached my miscreant, the deadbeat dad went along quietly.

———

Two years after Gregory was born we had another son, Brian Anthony. Now I was a father of two sons. Wow!

Barbara agreed with me that raising our kids was one of the most important jobs a person could have. She had worked a number of jobs before our first son was born but when Greg arrived, Barbara elected to be a stay-at-home mom. Neither of us has ever regretted that decision.

One day in the summer of 1973, I ran into Ed Reasor, the attorney who had employed me between the attorney general's office and the family court.

"Why don't you come back to work for me?" he suggested. Ed then made me an offer I couldn't refuse and I accepted. I was finally going into the private practice of law!

Chapter 26
Learning Experiences

Barbara and I learned early that driving in an Alaskan winter is a lot different from driving in a Wisconsin winter.

In November 1971 she and I, with our little son Greg, then one and a half years old, drove our Chevelle station wagon north from Anchorage. We planned to visit friends, Dick and Lucille Fredericks, who owned and operated Sportsmen's Paradise Lodge. The lodge is some twenty miles up the Nabesna Road, an old mining road off the main highway several hundred miles north of Anchorage.

We had several adventures on the way.

When Barbara was driving at Milepost 151 of the Glenn Highway, we hit a patch of black ice and sailed right off the road into a snowbank. It might be more accurate if I wrote that we sailed off the road *onto* a snowbank because we were going fast enough the car skimmed right over the snow, which was several feet deep, without sinking into it. Barbara let out a little yell as we shot at least ten feet off the road. She then calmly steered the car around the backside of the Milepost 151 sign and back onto the road. Had she hit the brakes, we would have slowed and sunk into the snow, but she handled the matter just right. When I took a picture of our car tracks later, I could not see how the car missed that milepost unless the sign itself dodged out of the way! My wife had done a wonderful bit of driving and, after taking the photos and thanking the Lord for our deliverance, we proceeded up the highway.

By the time we got to the beginning of the Nabesna Road, it was snowing heavily. At a place the locals refer to as "Dead Dog Hill," we had our second motoring adventure. I had failed to maintain sufficient forward momentum when I tried to drive up the hill. I had almost made it to the top when the car lost traction and we came to a stop. In backing down the hill, the car slid off the road and into a ditch. The car was resting at about a thirty-degree angle with its rear end about 5 feet off the road while the front end was almost on the road.

We got out of the car. It was very cold. Luckily I had packed some emergency gear before leaving town. Opening the tailgate, I got a bow saw and the car jack. I proceeded to cut a bunch of branches off a nearby tree, jack the car up, put the branches under the tires, and then let the car down on top of them. The car's weight would flatten the branches a bit, and then I'd repeat the process. After jacking the car up more than a dozen times, and cutting down several spruce trees in the process, I finally had the rear end of the car high enough so that it was level with the road.

Then it was just a matter of feathering the clutch and easing the Chevelle forward on the pile of branches until the car crawled back onto the road. Thank goodness the car had Posi-traction. The whole process of getting unstuck took almost three hours, and during that entire period not another car came along that road. Had I not been able to get us out of that ditch, it would have been a long cold night for the three of us.

By this time the snow was getting quite deep. I noticed that we began pushing snow with the front bumper as we advanced up the road. It was getting dark and the snow piled up in the front of the car. It began to cover the headlights, making it difficult to see where we were going. The snow was so deep it kept packing into the grill and I began worrying the car would overheat. As a result, we could drive only a few hundred yards at a time before I'd have to get out and clear away the snow from the head-lights and grill area.

When we finally pulled into the Sportsmen's Paradise parking lot, it was around 10 PM. The Fredericks had almost given up on us, and they said we were the first car that had driven as far as their lodge that whole day!

We had a nice visit with them over dinner and stayed overnight in one of their guest rooms. After breakfast the next morning, I went out to start the car. It started all right, but it refused to move. I couldn't get it to forward or backward. Dick Frederick figured he knew what the problem was. He crawled under the Chevelle and, using a blow torch, he thawed out the brake drums which had frozen to the wheels! That had never happened to me in the coldest winter in Wisconsin!

By now the Nabesna Road had been plowed and we headed south towards Anchorage. Late in the day, just south of Glennallen, we came to the Lake Louise Road.

———

Winter driving in Alaska wasn't the only adventure on that trip; I also learned what it meant to be on the wrong side of the law!

Game Unit 13 covers a large area called the Nelchina Basin, and begins eighty or ninety miles north of Anchorage. In the late 1960s and early 1970s a hunter could take up to four caribou each year and the caribou season ran from mid-August until the following March.

Today the caribou hunting there is designated a "subsistence" hunt, the limit is one caribou by drawing permit only, and the season lasts only a few weeks. Experts think that one of the reasons for the current decline in caribou numbers in that area is the abundance of snowmachines and off-road vehicles. Others attribute it to the large number of bears and wolves now roaming the area. But in the days of which I write, it was not unusual to see a herd of several hundred or more caribou cross the highway during hunting season. Whatever the reason, compared to the current day those were the good old days for caribou hunting.

Up until that day, I had gone caribou hunting several times after becoming an Alaska resident, but had not had any success.

I had heard the Lake Louise Road was a good place to hunt caribou so when we got to the cutoff, I suggested to Barbara we drive the road to see what we could see.

It was late in the day. About seven or eight miles in from the Glenn Highway I saw some fresh tracks showing that caribou had recently crossed the road. I knew I had only a short time to hunt so I suggested Barbara stay in the car while I followed the tracks and hunted a bit in the birch and spruce forest on the side of the road. "I'll be back before dark!" I promised.

Since the light was fading, I left my rifle in the car and took only my revolver, a S&W model 1950 target in .45 Colt. The landscape consisted of low rolling hills and it was easy walking so I went farther into the woods than I had intended. Just as I realized I would have to hustle back to keep my promise to Barbara, I spotted a caribou quietly standing behind a small, snow-covered bush about thirty-five yards away. It was an easy shot, and it took only one. I had bagged my first caribou!

Barbara, Greg, and Wayne Ross with Wayne's first caribou on the Lake Louise
Road near Glennallen, Alaska. We used this picture as our
Christmas picture at Christmas 1971.

I quickly field-dressed it but realized it was a long way to the car. There
certainly was no way I would make it back to the car with the caribou by
dark. In fact, there was no way I would be able to get the caribou back to
the car at all that night without a flashlight or lantern! So I tied my business card on the antlers and headed back to the road. By the time I got
there, Barbara was getting worried. But she had heard the shot and figured
I must have gotten something. She was just about to head into the woods
herself, with our little boy, to look for me.

We had arranged to stay at Rex and Shirley Close's vacant cabin at Mile 101 that night so just before we got to the cabin, I stopped at a roadhouse and called another friend, Jim Pressley. I told Jim about the caribou and asked if he wanted to drive up the next morning and help me pack the animal out to the car. I promised him a share of the meat if he helped and, good friend that he was, he readily agreed to do so.

Jim Pressley met us at the Closes' cabin the next morning and we all drove back to the Lake Louise Road. After parking the cars, Jim and I hiked into the woods and located my caribou. The ravens had clearly been to work but had not yet been very successful. Jim and I tied a rope on the caribou horns and started dragging it out of the woods. Later I learned how Alaskans cut animals up, a practice called "quartering." Real Alaskans would not have hauled a caribou as far as we did without quartering it. On the hike back to the cars, Jim asked me if I had "notched" my harvest ticket[15]. "Not yet," I responded. "I'll do it as soon as we get back to the car."

I should have listened to Jim. When we came out of the forest dragging my caribou, a State Fish and Game warden's car was parked behind mine. Fish & Game Officer Charles K_____ approached me and asked to see my hunting license which I showed him. Then he asked to see my harvest tag.

"I've still got to notch it," I explained.

"Too late!" he responded. Then he took out his citation book.

"What do you mean too late?" I protested. "I just got my caribou out of the woods! You saw me do it!"

It didn't help my case much when my buddy Pressley, at that moment, chose to blurt out to me "I *told* you to notch that tag!"

Despite my cajoling, and ignoring my reasoned arguments, Officer K_____ wrote out a citation for Failure to Notch a Harvest Tag, and handed it to me somewhat gleefully. "You'll have to appear in court in Glennallen on Thursday," he explained.

"Thursday! That's three days from now!" I protested. "Why can't we just go to court now?"

"Today is a holiday" Officer K_____ stated. (It was Alaska Day.) "The magistrate won't want to come to court on a holiday!"

"Let's go ask him," I suggested.

---

[15] A harvest ticket (also known as a "tag") is a small card on which the hunter is to cut a notch on the month and date of the kill. This insures that hunters will not take more caribou than the law allows.

"Not me!" Officer K_____ said. "I have to patrol this road today!"

"Well, you stay and patrol!" I growled at him. "I'm going to see the magistrate today!"

"You can't go without me!" Officer K_____ responded.

"Just watch me!" I growled back. "Come on Jim!" I motioned to Pressley. "We're going to Glennallen!"

Pressley got in the car with me and we headed for Glennallen, leaving Officer K_____ standing by the side of the Lake Louise Road. Finally realizing that I was serious and was heading for the magistrate in Glennallen, K_____ hopped in his patrol car and soon caught up and passed me. His car was parked outside the Fish & Game office in Glennallen when we got there. The magistrate's office and courthouse were next door.

"Are you going to call him or should I?" I asked Officer K_____ after walking into his office. Protesting that the magistrate would not be happy, K_____ called Magistrate Sheldon Sprecher, and Judge Sprecher agreed to come over. Meanwhile Officer K_____ was furiously typing up a formal complaint to the criminal charge of failing to notch a harvest tag.

It took Judge Sprecher only a few minutes to get to the courthouse. He put on his robe, called the court into session, and asked Officer K_____ to explain what was going on. Officer K_____ outlined the charge. I heard him mention the words "misdemeanor" and he recommended a fine of $100.

The magistrate then turned to me and said, "Now we'll hear from you, Mr. Ross, but first I want to advise you of your rights."

I told the magistrate I too worked for the court system. I fully understood my rights, and I waived his reading of them. "Now I want to move to dismiss this complaint!"

The magistrate asked, "Upon what grounds?" and I then proceeded to make my argument. I pointed out that the regulation said a person was to notch his harvest tag immediately upon taking an animal. The word "immediately" had to be interpreted as meaning "within a reasonably short time," however.

"Suppose you shot a caribou at a distance of 300 yards and it fell down. Do you immediately notch your harvest tag? What happens if the caribou then gets up and runs away? Now you have notched your harvest tag before you have taken a caribou. Have you violated the law by notching your tag too soon? Or what happens if, after shooting the caribou and seeing it fall 300 yards away, you walk to it to make sure it is dead? Arguably, in delaying the notching of your tag until you have walked the 300 yards to the fallen caribou, you again have broken the law by not notching the tag immediately. Thus, if immediately is defined as the very instant, problems can occur. It makes much more sense to interpret immediately as within a reasonably short time."

I argued this was my first caribou, I was excited, and so I had reason to be forgetful. I stated I had shot it with a handgun, I was just bringing it out of the woods, and I had not even reached my car on the road when cited. Had I tied the caribou on my car and was taking it home, I reasoned, there might be a better argument for a citation but getting the animal to my car, before notching, was "within a reasonably short time."

I then pointed out that the purpose of the harvest tag system was to prevent people from taking more caribou than allowed, the season allowed the taking of four caribou per year, this was my third year of hunting, and I had not gotten any caribou before this one. "I haven't taken too many caribou, Your Honor! In three years had I been lucky, I could have harvested a total of twelve. In fact, however, I've gotten only one! So rather than taking too many caribou, I'm actually eleven short!"

I argued that Officer K_____ could have accomplished far more in protecting the resource by giving a warning rather than by writing a ticket. Each fish and game officer is responsible for patrolling tens of thousands of miles of Alaska. The only way they can be even moderately successful is if they have the support of the general public. And writing tickets for minor violations simply alienates the general public, while a warning kindly given could cause a citizen to want to help such wardens in the future. I told the magistrate when I was with the Department of Law, we had trouble getting a guilty verdict from a jury, even in very serious fish and game cases because jurors simply did not like fish and game officers.

"And they don't like fish and game officers precisely because of actions like Officer K_____ took here today!" I said loudly, shaking my finger at Officer K_____.

Officer K_____ was angry! He got up and blustered. I wasn't sure just what he was saying but I thought he was now arguing for a $250 fine, rather than the $100 fine I heard earlier.

After patiently listening to Officer K_____, Magistrate Sprecher rendered his verdict.

"It's a holiday today! So case dismissed!"

Officer K_____ glared at me and then stormed out of the courtroom. As I was putting on my coat the magistrate invited me into his chambers.

"That K_____ is a problem!" he said. "He has no common sense." Magistrate Sprecher then told me about a case Officer K_____ had brought before his court the previous week.

A fellow had parked his car on the Lake Louise Road, and got out of the car when he saw a caribou a little ways off the road. He shot the caribou and dragged it to his car, and then dutifully notched his harvest ticket. He then put his wallet, containing his hunting license, into his glove compartment before beginning to field-dress the animal. Officer K_____ came along and asked to see the man's hunting license and the man said he'd have to get it out of his car, which was about twenty feet away.

"Officer K_____ actually gave the man a ticket for not having his hunting license in his possession!" Judge Sprecher groused.

"I dismissed that case too!" Sprecher continued, with a smile.

I thanked the magistrate for his courtesy and left the courtroom. He and I later became good friends and we still correspond, at least at Christmas, even after some forty plus years.

Barbara and I had an uneventful drive back to Anchorage.

A few days later I stopped in to see Buck Stewart, head of the state's fish and game division. I had first met him when I was with the Department of Law and we were working on the Al Burnette case and others. I told Buck my Officer K_____ story and suggested that "his guys" were still trying to make a federal case out of situations when a warning would be far more appropriate.

Buck agreed with me.

About six months later, Buck called and asked me to again stop by his office. When I got there he threw a small gold badge on the desk in front of me. "There's a present for you!" Buck stated. He continued "It's Officer K_____'s badge! We let him go last week. Despite our best efforts, he never got the word on how we wanted cases like yours handled. So I'm giving you his badge as a souvenir. Now you can say the only guy who ever tried to give you a ticket … well, you ended up with his badge!"

Chapter 27
Fast Eddie

Edward J. Reasor was one of Alaska's most colorful lawyers. Some called him "Fast Eddie" although probably not directly to his face, unless they were good friends of his. Others called him "the Calhoun." There was nothing shy about Ed in or out of court.

He was good to me and taught me a lot.

Ed Reasor had a number of idiosyncracies and sometimes his stories seemed so outrageous they simply couldn't be true … and yet I don't recall ever catching Fast Eddie in a whopper. Well, at least I didn't catch him very often. If he told whoppers, they stayed told. For example, Ed claimed he had been raised in an orphanage in Pennsylvania and that he had put himself through law school. At the orphanage, he said he was forced to eat everything on his plate. "If I didn't eat clean my plate at breakfast, I'd see the same food at lunch. If I didn't eat it at lunch, I'd see the same food at dinner! Now that I am on my own, I don't have to clean my plate, and I don't!" As a result, Ed always left a bit of food on his plate after eating, as if proving to himself that he was no longer at the orphanage.

Ed claimed he had met his second wife, Lilianne, during a year's sabbatical while living next door to Marlon Brando on a beach in Tahiti. Ed said Brando was filming *Mutiny on the Bounty* at the time. Lilianne was a beautiful Southeast Asian woman, who we privately called "The Dragon Lady" after the character in the cartoon strip *Terry and the Pirates* because she was tough and aggressive. When Lilianne was around, Fast Eddie pretty well toed the line.

In addition to his Anchorage office, Ed also claimed to have offices all over the world. His letterhead showed offices in Honolulu, Manila, and Singapore, among other exotic places.

When Ed hired me he promised I would be able to travel to some of the "outlying offices." I figured some trips to Hawaii or to the Far East would be fun. Instead, I found out the "outlying offices" Ed had in mind were somewhat closer to Anchorage than Honolulu or Manila.

The terms of the employment offer Ed Reasor made were interesting and imaginative.

I was to be an associate attorney in Ed's Anchorage office. I would be paid a salary for that work.

Ed also had a branch office in Seward, Alaska with two partners, Charles Tunley and Herb Ross[16]. Seward is a small fishing town about 100 miles by road southeast of Anchorage.

Ed also had a branch office in Cordova, another small fishing town about 100 miles east of Anchorage. I would be a named partner in the Cordova office.

I accepted Ed's offer.

I never did get to go to Ed's alleged offices in the Far East but I did get to go to Ed's Seward office once or twice and to the Cordova office regularly.

At that time, Ed had one other associate attorney, a fellow named Donald J. Miller. Coincidentally, Don Miller was from Milwaukee too, and like me, he had graduated from Marquette University law school. Don was from the class of 1958, while I was from the class of 1968.

Don was a former FBI agent. In his full-time job, he was co-ordinator for the criminal justice program at the University of Alaska-Anchorage (UAA). Don practiced law on a part-time basis. He was an expert at criminal motion practice. His motions were clear, concise, and straight to the point. When Don filed a motion, the court generally granted it.

Don seldom appeared at the office-so seldom we called him "the phantom." He held that nickname until the day he died. Some members of Ed Reasor's staff did not know who Don was when he'd walk into the office because he showed up so infrequently.

Don had the same deal I had; he was an associate in the Anchorage office and a partner in the Cordova office.

---

[16] Herb Ross was no relation to me. Both Tunley and Ross went on to become judges.

The three of us-Ed, Don, and I-were partners in what Ed Reasor called "our branch office". We shared, equally, the profits from the Cordova office. One of us would fly from Anchorage to Cordova on Friday morning, handle any legal work there, and fly back Friday night. If the fish were in or if the ducks were flying, we'd stay overnight in Cordova and go fishing or hunting there on Saturday. Then we'd fly back to Anchorage on Saturday night. Although we didn't make a lot of income from the branch office, we provided a service to the community, handled some interesting cases, and after paying office expenses we made enough each month so we each had a little walking-around money in our pockets.

———

Some of the stories about Ed Reasor have become classics.

On one occasion Ed had to make an unexpected appearance in Judge Moody's courtroom. Ed had failed to wear a necktie that morning and knew he was in trouble when Moody started rolling his eyes and began a long discourse on upholding the decorum of the court. As Moody rambled on, eyes closed, it was obvious the judge was working himself into a "mad-on." When Moody had a mad-on somebody was in serious trouble.

Ed knew Moody was preparing to monetarily sanction him for not wearing a tie in his court. As Moody droned on, Ed reached down below the counsel table, removed one of his shoelaces, and quickly tied it around his neck.

When Judge Moody finally completed his rambling monolog he muttered, "And Mr. Reasor, you will be sanctioned twenty-five dollars for failing to wear a tie in my courtroom!"

Ed stood up and said "Your Honor, I think there is some mistake! I am wearing a tie! It's one of those new string ties!" and Ed proudly pointed to the shoelace around his neck.

Moody, surprised, focused his eyes on Ed's neck. Seeing Ed's "string tie," Moody went on to state, "I am sorry, Mr. Reasor. I didn't notice that little tie of yours!"

The judge then reluctantly set aside the $25 sanction he had imposed for Ed not wearing a tie.

Ed was quite pleased with himself … until Moody then went on to sanction him $50 "for not having a shoelace in your shoe!"

Ed Reasor paid the fine. I think he figured it was worth $50 to be able to add that story to his repertoire.

———

Shortly thereafter, however, Ed purchased a powder blue leisure suit. He then had a big, colorful Mickey Mouse embroidered on the back of the suit jacket. Ed tried to always wear the suit when he went to Moody's court. Ed made sure, however, he never turned his back on the judge. As a result, Moody never saw the Mickey Mouse but everybody else in the courtroom did. Ed said his Mickey Mouse made a statement about his feelings in having to appear before Judge Moody.

———

There weren't a lot of women practicing law in those days. Ed had a jury trial one day and his opposing counsel was a very nice looking young female lawyer. Just after the jury was seated, Ed whispered to her "Sandie … what are we doing here? We should be across the street at the Captain Cook Hotel making mad, passionate love!" Ed then rolled his eyes.

The female attorney's face turned bright red and she was quite flustered. She continued to be flustered throughout the trial because every time she looked at Ed, he winked, rolled his eyes, or pointed in the direction of the hotel across the street. Ed had no problem winning the trial.

The next time Ed tried a case against that woman lawyer, she came into the courtroom and before Ed could say anything, the lady whispered in Ed's ear, "We *really should* be across the street at the Captain Cook", and then she rolled her eyes. Every time Ed looked at her during the ensuing trial the lady winked, rolled her eyes, or pointed in the direction of the Captain Cook. "I couldn't concentrate!" Ed complained later. "I lost the trial! Sandie beat me at my own game! I'll never try that trick again!" And to my knowledge, Ed never did.

———

One December, Ed announced that he was making a New Year's resolution for the firm.

"No more dog cases!" Ed stated. He defined a dog case as one in which the law was against us, or the damages were minimal, or liability was unclear. "We are going to stick with that resolution next year!" he ordered. "No more dog cases! Only apple pie cases next year!"

As Ed told the story later, shortly after the first of the year a good-looking young woman came in to see him. She had been thrown out of a bar, allegedly for being rowdy, and she wanted to sue the bartender.

Uh-oh! Ed thought. A dog case! And we had just made a resolution to not take any more dog cases. So Ed began making excuses why he could not take the lady's case; we were too busy; we had a potential conflict; and so forth.

Then the lady took her coat off. "She had a dress cut down the front to her navel!" Ed exclaimed. "Her case instantly started to look better to me! ... But then I remembered my New Year's resolution. So I reluctantly turned down the case!"

But the lady's dress was so spectacular that Ed thought, Whose day can I brighten by referring this lady to them? Then he thought of Bill E. Bill E. was an attorney who had been practicing law since Peter was pope and Bill had been married to the same woman almost that entire time. Bill and his wife had a bunch of kids of varying ages. Bill could use some excitement! Ed thought, so he referred the lady with the spectacular dress to attorney Bill E. "Bill E. is the best attorney you can get in these kinds of cases!" Ed assured the woman.

A week or so later, Ed ran into Bill E. at the courthouse. Ed asked Bill if the lady he had referred to Bill ever had come in to see him.

"Oh, yes," Bill responded. "What a dog case! No law on her side! Few damages! And there appears to be little liability! Initially I decided not to take her case ... but then she took her coat off!"

———

Ed Reasor and Associates had its Anchorage office in a little yellow house at 4337 West Spenard Road in a portion of town called Spenard. Spenard was an older part of the city and somewhat notorious. A "Spenard Divorce," for example, referred to any incident when one spouse killed the other. At that time, Spenard had more massage parlors and sporting houses than any other part of town.

To the east of our office was a three-story building in which Lilianne Reasor had a shop on the first two floors. Her business was called *The Pagoda* and Lilianne sold Oriental and South Pacific furniture, toys, jewelry, and other items. Her shop was a lot like the *Pier One Imports* stores seen today in many cities. (Currently, the building holds Gwennie's Restaurant, one of Anchorage's more popular eating establishments.)

It was easy to tell what items were not selling well in Lilianne's shop. Those were the items the law office associates and secretaries received as Christmas gifts that year.

On the third floor of the Pagoda building, there was an apartment. The apartment was rented by a corporation known as the *Nevada Junketeers*. The *Junketeers* corporation was owned and run by one of Ed's clients. The corporation's stated purpose was to teach folks how to gamble "Las Vegas-style." I understand that classes were held most nights in the third-floor apartment. Of course gambling, as done in Las Vegas, was not legal in Alaska. As a result, once a month or so, the *Nevada Junketeers* chartered an airplane and flew its students to Las Vegas so they could try out what they had learned from the nightly classes on the third floor.

I was always a bit suspicious of the whole deal. To get to the apartment, there was a narrow steel door on the side of the Pagoda building at the parking lot level. There was a video camera above the door so that, presumably, the folks inside could see who was intending to come in and get "educated." Inside that steel door there was a narrow wooden stairway, one person wide. The stairway went up two flights to a small landing in front of another steel door leading to the third-floor apartment. The third-floor landing was so tiny there was not enough room to swing a battering ram; protection just in case someone felt the need to swing such a device to make a forced entry to the nightly classes.

I got up to the third-floor apartment one evening when "classes" were not in session. There was a fully stocked kitchen and bar, a huge "living room," and a large bathroom with jade countertops and gold fixtures. Even a bidet.

The apartment had one bedroom with a heart-shaped bed, substantially mirrored. Since I had gotten my education at Catholic facilities, I had never before seen such accouterments. I wondered about the kind of "education and training" the *Nevada Junketeers* were getting in that apartment.

Ed Reasor enjoyed the great outdoors of Alaska (circa 1975).

At the rear of the apartment was a balcony overlooking a small yard. The yard was completely surrounded by a twelve-foot-high wooden fence. On the balcony was a rope ladder. I was told that the rope ladder was for "fire escape purposes" or for "other emergencies." I also learned if a person really wanted to leave the night classes, without using the regular stairway, he could climb down the rope ladder, and knowing which slats on the fence to push, get through the fence and disappear into the neighboring trailer park.

I never took Las Vegas gambling lessons from the *Nevada Junketeers*. I don't think I could have afforded them.

———

Most self-respecting attorneys had offices downtown. Only a few of us operated from offices in the outlying areas like Spenard.

Alaska had a bar association. Anchorage, too, had a bar association. The City of Fairbanks had a bar association. Juneau, and even Kenai, had a bar association. Ed Reasor decided that Spenard should also have a bar association.

So we formed one.

Attorney Steve DeLisio became the first president of the Spenard Bar Association and I became its first vice president. Ed Reasor was, if I recall, the first and only treasurer. We had certificates printed up that said "Member of the Spenard Bare Assn." The e in the word <u>Bare</u> had an <u>x</u> superimposed over it. The <u>n</u> in <u>Assn</u> was printed smaller than the rest of that word. So the certificate looked, at first glance, like it was a certificate for membership in the "Spenard Bare Ass." It had a picture on it of a matronly lady loading a double-barreled shotgun. Each attorney who signed up for membership got one of those certificates. I still have mine somewhere. They probably are now collector's items.

The Spenard Bar Association had regular meetings in the old Gold Rush Hotel on Northern Lights Boulevard. We advertised our meetings and tried to get good speakers. When we had a good speaker we could have twenty-five to thirty attorneys attend from all over the city. When we didn't have good speakers, there'd be only four or five of us.

Ed Reasor was a movie buff. One day, when we were plotting activities for the Spenard Bar, Ed came up with the idea for a "Peter Sellers Film Festival." He had access to several Seller films-I think one of them was *The Pink Panther*. At that time, the Alaska Supreme Court had just moved into its quarters in the then new courthouse at 303 K Street. Somehow Ed arranged for the Spenard Bar Association to hold its "First Annual Peter Sellers Film Festival" in the large new Supreme Court courtroom.

We advertised the film festival heavily amongst the legal professionals. We had our wives make gallons of buttered popcorn. When the night arrived, the ladies sold soft drinks and popcorn at a table set up just outside the fifth-floor courtroom. A large crowd attended and everybody had a great time.

On Monday morning, the Supreme Court justices saw their new courtroom. They were not amused to find popcorn and soft drink bottles strewn around the room. There were not so veiled threats of charging the Spenard Bar Association with the janitorial costs to clean up the mess. With the Supreme Court obviously angry with the Spenard Bar Association, few attorneys wanted to even admit they were members. As a result, the Spenard Bar Association faded into history.

To the best of my knowledge, the Supreme Court justices never again allowed their courtroom to be used for anything other than court activities. Certainly, there are only a few of us still around who can brag that we ate popcorn in the Alaska Supreme Court courtroom!

———

As I wrote above, Ed Reasor loved movies. He gathered together some like-minded folks and formed a group he called "Cinema Cynics." Once a month or so the Cinema Cynics met at one or another's home to watch movies. Those were the days before video cassettes and DVDs, so that month's host or hostess would go down to Pictures Inc., pore through its catalog, and pick out a movie or two. If Pictures Inc. didn't have the movie, they'd order it for you.

For a nominal sum the host or hostess then rented the movie and a 16mm projector and screen, and when it was shown, the Cynics cheered or booed the action, the actors, the movie itself, or often all three. Drinks and snacks were served including, of course, the popcorn.

I can remember seeing movies like *Gunga Din, The Third Man, Witness for the Prosecution,* and other great classics.

Those get-togethers were in Fast Eddie's "drinking days" and whenever we met at his house, he usually fell asleep on the floor during the movie. Eventually the Dragon Lady covered him with a blanket and when the film was over, we'd all quietly leave so as not to disturb our sleeping host.

Chapter 28
Practicing at Reasor and Associates

I handled my first jury trial while working with Ed Reasor. Just like some people believe the best way to teach kids to swim is to throw them into the water, Ed apparently felt I should learn about jury trials by handling one.

One Friday morning Ed handed me a file about four inches thick. "This case is set for a jury trial on Monday morning in Fairbanks," he stated. "I want you to go up and try the case!" He was giving me three days to prepare. It was sink or swim!

Although I had met the client, I knew absolutely nothing about the case, and I told Ed so. "There are three other plaintiff lawyers," he explained. "We represent the fourth plaintiff. I've told the other plaintiff attorneys this would be your first jury trial so they agreed that you can go last with our portion of the case. It will be easy! All you have to do is do what they do, and pick up any crumbs, in the way of questioning the witnesses, that may need picking up after the other lawyers get through with their questions."

I immediately got to work reading the file. It involved an explosion and fire in an apartment building in Fairbanks. One moment our client had been asleep in his bed in his room. The next moment he found himself still in bed, but outside in the parking lot suffering serious injuries. Other tenants had also been injured. One lady had been killed.

Our client and the other injured parties, including the deceased woman's estate, sued the apartment owner. It appeared to all of us that the owner had intentionally caused the explosion to collect on insurance. Traces of dynamite were found in the rubble. And only two days before, all the fire doors and extinguishers had been removed from the building, ostensibly for renovations.

We had to walk a fine line. If we actually proved that the owner had set the fire or caused the explosion, the insurance company would refuse to cover the damages because of the owner's intentional conduct. So, to keep the insurance coverage, we had to prove the owner was negligent.

I flew to Fairbanks and rented a car. At trial Anchorage attorney David Thorsness represented the apartment building's owner. Dave, of course, had been hired by the insurance company. The other plaintiffs were represented by three Fairbanks lawyers, whose names are best untold. After we picked a jury the Fairbanks attorneys were quite pleased with themselves. One of them told me one juror was his mailman. "I always give my mailman a big tip for Christmas!" he explained. "If the guy expects another big tip this year, he'd better vote our way!"

The trial lasted several weeks. Most of the time I stayed in Fairbanks at various hotels. Rooms were hard to find then because of the Pipeline Boom[17]. I'd be able to stay in one hotel for a few days, and then had to move because the room had been reserved previously by guys coming in from the pipeline camps.

One time I made a reservation by phone, and after getting to the motel, I was given a key to my room. When I unlocked the door to the room, I was greeted by the sound of snoring. I went back to the front desk and complained that someone was sleeping in my room. The clerk told me that if I didn't like it, I could go somewhere else. I didn't, and I did.

During the entire time I spent in Fairbanks I never got invited out to dinner, or even for a drink, by my co-counsels, the Fairbanks attorneys. I didn't even get invited to go to lunch with them, ever. Neither did Dave Thorsness. Instead Dave and I, strangers in a strange land, ended up going to dinner together almost every night we were in Fairbanks. Dave was a delightful guy and a fine attorney.

After a trial that seemed to last forever, we made our final arguments and the case was turned over to the jury. The jury came back in about forty-five minutes with a defense verdict, finding for the apartment building owner. I had lost my first jury trial. What made it worse was that

---

[17] The Pipeline Boom was the period in the 1970s when the Trans-Alaska pipeline was being constructed from the Alaska's North Slope to Valdez. It was one of the biggest construction projects in history and attracted tens of thousands of workers from all over the United States.

during their forty-five minutes of deliberations, the jury had even sent out for lunch!

So much for a Christmas bonus for the mailman!

———

Patricia Carlin (not her real name) was a legal secretary in a state in mid-America. After dating Art Williams (not his real name), an attorney and coworker, Pat learned she was pregnant. Unfortunately by the time Pat learned she was "with child," Art had moved to Alaska, where he opened a law practice. Pat traveled to Anchorage to give Art the good news of his pending fatherhood. Unfortunately, Art was less than overjoyed and refused to have anything to do with Pat.

Pat, pregnant and broke, went to one of the social agencies. To make a long story short, Reasor and Associates ended up with a temporary legal secretary, eight months pregnant, and I ended up with a paternity case to handle.

I sent Art a nice letter requesting support for Pat "during her period of confinement" as we called pregnancy in those days. I also asked Art to pay Pat's medical bills and $150 a month child support after the baby was born. Art ignored me so I filed a paternity action against him.

Art hired Wendell Kay as his attorney. Known as the "Silver Fox," Wendell was considered one of the finest lawyers in Alaska. Wendell looked like a Southern patrician and was usually quite reserved and polite. My paternity case looked like it was going to develop into quite a battle. Pat eventually gave birth to a beautiful little girl. A day or two after the birth, I drafted a pleading which read something like this:

NOTICE OF PRODUCTION OF EXHIBIT A

To the Defendant and His Attorney Wendell Kay
PLEASE TAKE NOTICE that the plaintiff, Patricia Carlin, through her own labors and the able-bodied assistance of the defendant nine months ago, has now produced Exhibit A, more particularly described as:

Baby Girl Carlin
Exhibit A can be viewed by the defendant by making arrangements through his attorney. The plaintiff and her counsel send heartiest congratulations to the defendant upon the birth of his daughter.

In the center of this pleading was a colored photograph of Baby Girl Carlin in all her glory. I filed the pleading in the court clerk's office, and sent a copy to Wendell.

The next morning Wendell Kay called me. "You son-of-a-bitch!" were the first words from this usually elegant man. Wendell then proceeded to tell me what a fuss my Notice of Production of Exhibit A had caused. Apparently, the clerks at the courthouse thought it was a funny pleading, and that the baby's picture was cute. As a result, the clerks copied my pleading and sent it to other clerks in the courthouse. Art Williams could not go anywhere in the courthouse without seeing his daughter's picture posted on the wall, or on a railing, or on a door. And every place Art went the clerks pointed him out to other clerks as the alleged father of "that baby in the picture on the wall." And then the clerks laughed. It was the laughter that had gotten to Art Williams.

Wendell Kay and I settled that paternity case almost immediately. The settlement was for more than I had asked for originally.

Art Williams has never spoken to me since.

Wendell Kay died soon thereafter. That case was one of the few we ever had together.

Several years ago, Patricia Carlin called me. She was living in the Lower 48 and was married to a lawyer. Baby Girl Carlin was now in college, and Patricia wanted to let me know things were fine. She stated that Art had become a "pretty good dad," he had always paid his child support on time, and had even come down for their daughter's high school graduation. Patricia thanked me for representing her those long years ago. I thanked her for the call.

————

Ed Reasor, Don Miller, and I almost had an adventure that would have made a great movie script.

Alan Wayne Hurley had been arrested and charged with theft of a generator from Elmendorf Air Force Base. Hurley escaped from the Anchorage jail by hitting a guard with a serving tray. The Anchorage police, the Alaska State Troopers and even the FBI were all looking for him. Hurley fled to the Chitna area and his pursuers received a tip that he was hiding out at the Silver Lake Lodge.

After getting a search warrant from Magistrate Sheldon Sprecher of Glennallen, the troopers conducted an early-morning raid on the lodge.

Hurley wasn't there but one of the patrons, under questioning, revealed that Hurley was camped about a half mile away near the shore of Silver Lake. The magistrate and at least one or more troopers flew down the lake in a helicopter to look for Hurley and spotted a small tent. As they flew over the tent, Hurley popped out and began firing at the helicopter. Magistrate Sprecher responded in kind with a .44 Magnum he had been packing. A number of shots were fired by both sides but nobody was hit and Hurley fled into the woods.

Hurley was known to be an excellent woodsman, proficient in the use of firearms. Although an extensive search was conducted in the Chitna-McCarthy area, an area which later became the Wrangell-Saint Elias National Park, Hurley eluded everybody.

One day some rough-looking guys in motorcycle jackets came to our office. They were from a local motorcycle gang and they advised they knew where Hurley was. They had even been in contact with him. They advised that Hurley wanted to surrender but believed that he would be shot by the authorities if he tried to do so. To protect himself, Hurley wanted an attorney to accompany him when he turned himself in. So far no problem. One hitch, though, was that Hurley was staying at a cabin, with a girlfriend, a two-day ride by horseback from the nearest road.

Hurley wanted his attorney to get the law enforcement authorities to pull back a bit. He wanted his attorney to ride in to the cabin on horseback, pick up Hurley, and then ride back to an airstrip where the law was to be waiting. Don Miller, being a former FBI man himself, contacted the FBI and the Bureau agreed that they would hold back if we could bring Hurley in.

The second hitch was that Hurley did not want anyone, including his attorney(s), to be armed when they rode in to get him. It sounded like an interesting adventure but that "unarmed" bit didn't sit right with either Ed or me. Just in case we actually took on the Hurley matter, I purchased a lightweight S&W Centennial .38 revolver and had holster maker Bob Levine make me an ankle holster. I did not intend to go in possible harm's way without a "piece" and neither did Ed.

While arrangements were being made for his surrender, Hurley apparently developed cold feet. That, or his proposed surrender was just an attempt to buy him some time from the law. Whatever the reason, Hurley allegedly escaped by fleeing east, across the White River into Canada. He was a fugitive for nine years.

On one occasion law enforcement located Hurley in wild country near Eugene, Oregon. He was believed to be hiding in a wooded canyon across a river from the nearest road. Early in the morning while it was still dark officers waded across the river-which they described as "extremely cold." As they approached the area where Hurley was believed to be camped, they narrowly avoided stepping into a "snake pit" which Hurley had dug to ambush pursuers. There were fifteen to twenty rattlesnakes in the pit. In what was described as a "shoot-out in the wilderness" Hurley again escaped. He became somewhat of a folk hero.

Hurley eventually made it to the US Marshal's Fifteen Most Wanted Fugitives List. He finally was arrested in Bellingham, Washington without incident. He was living with a girlfriend in a small house with a $400,000 marijuana-growing operation in the crawl space. He was extradited to Alaska.

The law office of Edward J. Reasor and Associates never represented Alan Wayne Hurley nor, in fact, did we ever even meet him. But even dealing with potential clients in Ed's office was an interesting experience.

Chapter 29

Outdoor Adventures at Reasor and Associates

One day Ed Reasor asked me what would be a good rifle caliber for moose hunting.

I told Ed a lot of hunters in Alaska use and swear by the .338 Winchester Magnum.

"What grain bullet would a moose hunter use?" Ed asked.

I suggested a 180-grain bullet.

"What's the average distance at which a person might shoot a moose?" Ed asked.

I told Ed moose often are shot at fifty yards or less.

Ed carefully wrote down each one of my answers and then asked the same questions about caliber, bullet weight, and distance for shooting a caribou. Again he carefully wrote down my answers.

When Ed repeated the same questions about shooting a sheep, and once again carefully wrote down my responses, I was curious. I asked why he wanted that information. He muttered something about "a research project."

A few months later, a friend of mine came back from a visit to Hawaii. My friend said while he was in Honolulu, he had stopped in to visit a law office Ed Reasor maintained there. "Fast Eddie must be quite a hunter!" my friend casually remarked.

"Why do you say that?" I asked.

"Well," my friend replied, "Ed's got a big moose rack on the wall with a sign that says 'Killed by Edward J. Reasor with a Winchester .338 rifle, using a 180-grain bullet, at a distance of fifty yards.' There's a big caribou with a sign stating what caliber of rifle he used to shoot the caribou, listing bullet weight and distance. And he's got a big set of sheep horns, with similar information! His clients in Honolulu are quite impressed!"

I found out later Ed had obtained some mounted game heads, perhaps as part of a fee or as a gift from someone. He then shipped the trophies to his Hawaiian office and mounted them on the walls. But he wanted to sound knowledgeable about rifles, calibers, and distances. I suddenly realized why he had pumped me for information about typical calibers, bullet weights, and shooting distances! He wanted to put such information on signs under each game head so it would look like Ed had taken those trophies!

"It was good for business!" Ed explained.

––––––

Despite taking credit in Hawaii for someone else's hunting trophies, Ed managed to get out and experience the Alaskan out-of-doors himself, although not as often as he wished. In addition to being an excellent attorney, he was a good boss and a generous man. On one occasion for example, after Ed had settled a client's personal injury case and earned a nice contingent fee, he announced he was going to take all the attorneys in the office on a fishing trip. Ed delegated me to choose the destination.

Chuck and Carol Petersen were longtime friends. They lived around the corner from the duplex Barbara and I had built at 1326 P Street. Chuck's dad, Ray Petersen, was an Alaskan pioneer aviator and he owned a local airline, Wien Air Alaska. Wien was the concessionaire at Katmai National Monument on the Alaska Peninsula, several hundred air miles south and west of Anchorage. I had often heard Chuck talk about the various fishing camps he and his brother Sonny ran there for their dad.

Wien's biggest and best-known camp was at the Brooks River, a world-famous fishing stream where the fishermen often share the fishing with Alaskan brown bears. But Wien had a second, smaller camp in Katmai, Grosvernor Camp. I talked to Chuck about Reasor and Associates coming to Katmai to go fishing. Chuck stated the fishing at Grosvernor Camp would be almost as good as at Brooks Camp. I chose Grosvernor Camp as our destination when Chuck assured me we would have Grosvernor to ourselves, except for a fishing guide and a cook.

In 1912 Mount Katmai, a large volcano in that area, exploded in one of the most violent volcanic explosions in recorded history. More than 3,000 square miles surrounding Mount Katmai were blanketed by ash deposits a foot or more thick. After the National Geographic Society sent expeditions to Katmai and reported its findings, even calling one place *the Valley of Ten Thousand Smokes,* President Woodrow Wilson named the Katmai area a national monument in 1918.

In recent years Katmai has been declared a national park, although it was still a national monument when we of Reasor and Associates traveled there for what Ed called "a law office retreat."

We flew a Wien Airlines commercial jet to King Salmon and then climbed aboard a Wien Grumman Mallard, a large amphibious airplane like a Grumman Goose on steroids. The Mallard could land on land or water, had twin engines, and carried up to seventeen passengers. That trip was the only time I ever flew in a Mallard and it was quite an airplane. We landed in the water at Grosvernor and taxied up to the beach.

Grosvenor Camp was situated on a low glacial moraine overlooking a water channel connecting Lake Colville and Lake Grosvenor. Both lakes have excellent salmon, rainbow, and grayling fishing.

We all had a wonderful time. After breakfast we'd walk a few dozen feet to the channel between the lakes and fish until lunch. We'd eat a great lunch cooked by the Wien chef and then, after a nice nap, we'd fish until supper. After another gourmet meal, we'd return to the lodge and play poker and drink whiskey until it was time for bed. Ed made us all promise we would not talk about our cases, or anything else of a legal nature, and we did our best to keep that promise.

The fishing was fabulous! We caught fish until our arms ached. Generally salmon or rainbows.

The rainbows ranged from fifteen to twenty-two inches in length, and it was "catch and release" for the most part.

Ed had decided we ought to organize a betting pool for the largest fish caught during the trip. Since we were catching so many salmon, they would not be eligible for entry in winning the pool. Each of us threw in five dollars. Every day somebody would claim to have caught a fish larger than anyone had caught the day before.

Ed claimed to have the record with a twenty-five inch rainbow and try as we might, none of us could catch anything (other than salmon) bigger than Ed's fish. Of course, none of us had seen Ed's twenty-five inch fish! But Ed assured us he had caught such a fish and then released it! And who were we to question the veracity of the guy who was footing the bills?

One day I got tired of hearing Ed's bragging and I took the guide aside. "What other fish do you have in this lake?" I asked him. He told me from time to time someone had caught six- or even eight-pound northern pike in a little bay at the eastern end of Grosvernor Lake.

"Let's go!" I told the guide. "I used to know how to catch northerns when I lived in Wisconsin. An eight pound northern should be bigger than Ed's claimed twenty-five inch rainbow!"

The guide took me by boat up the lake and into a weedy, shallow bay. It looked like a haven for northern pike, and it was. Unfortunately it was so weedy our casts generally resulted in large strands of weeds rather than fish.

Then I found an old, well-worn Johnson Silver Minnow spoon in the bottom of my tackle box. I had used that bait successfully for northerns in Wisconsin. But in Wisconsin we had a jar of what was called "pork rind." Pork rind was white and about two inches long. We would clip the pork rind to the weedless hook of the Johnson Silver Minnow and when the lure was retrieved, the pork rind rippled enticingly along. Pork rind always seemed to drive northerns wild.

Unfortunately, I didn't have any pork rind at Grosvenor Camp. So, in lieu of pork rind, I tied a strip of a red handkerchief and a strip of a white handkerchief onto the Silver Minnow's hook and cast it out into the biggest weed bed I could see. The weedless hook on my lure allowed the silver spoon to slither along the top of the weeds, while the colored handkerchief strips rippled behind.

Suddenly there was a mighty splash and a huge, toothed mouth came up out of the weeds and scooped up my bait. "My God, it's an alligator!" the guide yelled.

When I finally got the fish into the boat, it was a thirty-nine inch, sixteen pound northern pike. I knew it was bigger than anything Fast Eddie had caught. It was even bigger than anything he could hope to catch! So I kept that fish.

For the next hour or two we caught northerns on almost every cast. I kept only one more fish, a thirty-one incher that must have weighed around ten pounds.

On my last cast of the afternoon, I latched on to a really big northern. We got the fish to the boat, and measured and weighed it. It was forty-four inches long and weighed some twenty pounds. I remembered having heard somewhere big northerns grow two inches in length a year, so a twenty pounder was a pretty old fish. Since I had taken one large northern, the sixteen pounder, I didn't want to kill another. I let the big one go, but I took his picture as he swam off in the clear green water.

The author and his prize-winning 39 inch Northern Pike at
Grosvernor Lake, Alaska (circa 1975).

When we got back to camp that afternoon, I held up the smaller of
my two fish. "Get your money out, Ed!" I chortled. "This thirty-one inch
northern is bigger than your twenty-five inch rainbow."

I was not surprised, however, to hear Ed claim that while I had a nice
fish, he had caught a bigger one. "This afternoon I caught a thirty-three
inch rainbow!" Ed responded. "My thirty-three inch rainbow is bigger
than your thirty-one inch northern!"

When we all asked to see Ed's big rainbow he, of course, claimed to
have released it. Everyone but me expressed their disbelief in Ed's claim.

"I believe him!" I said to the crowd. "If Ed says his biggest fish was a thirty-three inch rainbow, I trust Ed to tell the truth!"

Ed beamed, looked around, and nodded his head in agreement.

"Unfortunately, Ed," I continued, "your thirty-three inch rainbow isn't as big as my thirty-nine inch northern!" I slowly slid my bigger fish out from under the seat of the boat and held it up. Ed gulped and finally had to agree I had won the pool with the largest fish.

"You think that is a nice fish?" I continued. "You should have seen the forty-four incher I caught and released!

We all had a good laugh that evening because I had beaten Ed at his own game.

A day or two later, Ed and several of the other fellows expressed an interest in seeing Brooks Camp. They flew there for the day while I stayed at Grosvernor with one or two other guys. That evening when Ed and his group got back to Grosvernor, I heard Ed mutter to the other guys "Don't you dare tell him! His head is big enough as it is!"

As soon as I could, I got one of the more junior associates alone and leaned on him a bit." "Don't tell me what?" I insisted.

I finally got the associate to reveal what Ed had tried to conceal. According to the associate, when Ed and his group got to Brooks Camp they came across a new book called *Exploring Katmai National Monument and the Valley of Ten Thousand Smokes*. On page 175 of the book, there were a few paragraphs about northern pike. One of them stated:

Alaska's trophy-fish award program recognizes pike larger than fifteen pounds (6.8 kg). Without question, monument waters contain pike of this size, though none have yet been reported ...

My buddy, Ed Reasor, hadn't wanted anyone to tell me that my pool-winning sixteen pound northern pike was the largest northern ever reported caught in Monument waters up to that time!

No wonder they called him Fast Eddie!

———

Another of my adventures with Fast Eddie was a sheep hunt at Lake Clark. Lake Clark National Park and Preserve is located southwest of Anchorage. The area became a national park during the Carter Administration when Jimmy Carter locked up tens of thousands of acres of Alaska, closing much of it to hunting. To this day I dislike President Carter immensely.

Lake Clark itself lies in a northeast to southwest direction. It is some forty plus miles long and is surrounded by mountains. I worked at Reasor and Associates before Lake Clark became a national park and one fall we went on a Dall sheep hunt there.

I knew a pilot by the name of Larry Thompson and sought Larry's advice on where might be a good place to hunt the mountain sheep. Larry suggested the south shore of the upper end of Lake Clark. That area was known as Little Lake Clark. "There is a canyon on the south shore that goes back several miles. No one has hunted the area in years and when I've flown over the area, I've always seen sheep!" Larry stated. "Even better, it is a gradual walk to the sheep because there is a nice game trail on the eastern side of the canyon."

Larry arranged for a guide friend of his, Rick Burnham, to accompany us. The fourth member of the party was District Court Judge Joseph Brewer[18]. I had mentioned the planned trip to the judge one day and he indicated he'd like to go along. From Larry's description of the country, it could not be too difficult a hunt and we each hoped to have nice rams on our office walls for only a few days of exercise.

Larry took off from Anchorage's Lake Hood in his well-used Cessna 180 floatplane. Rick, our gear, and I were on the first flight. As we flew over Cook Inlet, we saw some of the fourteen offshore oil platforms, gas flares showing they were busily pumping oil. Then we flew over the duck flats on the west side of the Inlet, and eventually made the dogleg through Lake Clark Pass. All too soon the plane settled down on the calm, blue-green lake and coasted up to the rocky shore.

Rick and I set up our big tent while Larry went back for Ed and Joe. Our base camp was near the lake and several hundred feet from where the canyon began. While waiting for Larry and the other guys, I caught a couple of lake trout for supper. Joe wrote, later, "A delightful repast, cooked over a driftwood fire, completed the evening."

We kidded each other about being out of shape but we were all confident we could make the long climb up the canyon, and then up to the

---

[18] Joe Brewer wrote an unpublished manuscript of our trip, *Ordeal in Sheep Country*, from which I've borrowed extensively to refresh my memory about events over three decades past. Thanks Joe! I only wish you were still here to see some of your writing finally in print.

peaks, some of which reached 4,000 to 5,000 feet. We were all Alaska residents, and we knew that a sheep hunt involved something more than walking up a grassy slope, bagging a ram, and then walking down again. But none of us foresaw the rugged ordeal we'd endure.

That night we were all awakened by a bear snorting and snuffling near the tent, but our shouts and my flashlight frightened it off.

Early the next morning we started our long trek up the canyon, scrambling over boulders and through alder brush near the creek for the first hundred yards. We could not seem to locate the "nice game trail on the east side of the canyon" Larry had promised. In fact, we could not seem to locate any game trails at all!

Although our backpacks had been somewhat lightened by leaving many nonessentials at the base camp, we still carried two small tents, cooking and eating utensils, several tiny one-burner gasoline stoves and fuel for cooking, three or four days' worth of freeze, dried food, matches in waterproof containers, dry socks, sweaters, ponchos, and sundry small items for quick energy snacks. We had cameras, canteens, binoculars, and sleeping bags. Joe had a Winchester Model 70 .30-06 rifle and a S&W .357 Magnum revolver; Ed had a Browning bolt action .338 rifle and a Ruger .44 Magnum revolver; Rich had a Sako .30-06 rifle, and I had a BSA .30-06 rifle and a S&W revolver in .45 Long Colt.

After 300 yards we abandoned the creek bottom as the walking was too rough. Of course, it didn't help the walking either when we came to a two-hundred-foot waterfall a short distance up the creek. We had to do a lot of rock climbing to reach the next section of the canyon above it. Even side-hilling was tough. The alders were thick and snagged our backpacks, clothing, weapons, and boots. Stepping on an alder branch growing close to the ground insured a fall, for the bark was slippery even when dry. Grabbing an alder branch was dangerous too for it often broke loose in our hands. In many places, tall grass and ferns obscured the ground. Thorns on the waist-high devil's club plants tore at our hands and made us glad we had brought heavy leather gloves.

Above the falls we again entered the creek bed and kept climbing. Even walking on rocks and boulders at the edge of the creek was dangerous. The cold swift water, ankles to knees in depth, made treacherous footing. Many large boulders, higher than a man's head, had to be clambered over. Around a series of these, a swaying alder branch knocked Joe's glasses into the creek and they disappeared instantly downstream. Fortunately

Joe had brought along a pair of prescription sunglasses, without which he would have been severely handicapped.

After some nine hours of climbing we had gained only about 1,800 feet in elevation. Looking down the canyon, we could see where we had started, only a mile or two away in a straight line. Yet we estimated we had walked about six miles, almost all of it uphill.

Overnight camp was made about mid-afternoon on a narrow sloping ledge. The ground was somewhat rocky but there were grasses and varieties of mountain flowers everywhere there was enough soil to permit their growth.

Late in the day Rick set off to see if he could get high enough to spot sheep. He was gone five hours, returning just before dark. He hadn't seen sheep, but he had seen something else. He had worked his way up to a basin where Larry had said he sometimes had seen rams from the air. Rick was standing on a slope of fifty-five to sixty degrees, leaning forward for balance, as he reached out to pick some large blueberries when he heard a loud roar. Startled, Rick looked up to see a black bear rushing down the hill at him. Rick was just able to raise his rifle and fire from the hip at the bear and jump out of the way. The bear hurtled past him, head over paws, coming to rest some two hundred feet down the slope. Rick's one hurried shot had found its mark and killed the bear instantly.

"That's the first time in my years of guiding that I've been attacked by a black bear" Rick said later. "Generally they will run away from a man!" A second black bear feeding in the same area, stood up at the shot, Rick reported. But the rifle blast apparently frightened it and it scurried up the mountain rather than attacking.

It had been quite a day and though we were tired, we were all in good spirits. We had seen no sheep but had spotted bears all day, high on the slopes. We had a hearty meal. We just knew we were now in sheep country. We looked upon Rick's bear as just an advance bonus to our hunt.

The next morning, leaving our erected tent as a spike camp, we pushed on up the canyon. Ed went up one side of the canyon while Rick and I left the creek bed on the other side and worked our way upslope to Rick's bear. As we dressed it out we began to spot sheep high in basins or on almost vertical craggy slopes, but only ewes and lambs. No rams. But we did see a grizzly sow with two cubs. We were glad they were a long way off. We concluded the rams must be further up the canyon. Late that afternoon we rendezvoused with Ed and Joe.

Rather than going down the canyon to our spike camp we decided to stay where we were that night and climb higher the next day. Joe set up our one remaining tent, sharing it with Rick while Ed and I slept in our sleeping bags under the stars, hands on our rifles. No bears came into camp that night but in the morning fresh tracks in a patch of sand showed one had approached after dark within 150 yards of our tent.

Our sheep hunt began in earnest that morning. Although the slopes and hogback ridges spilling from the high peaks were steep, the walking was easier. We were now well above treeline. As a consequence, the alders were stunted and much less of a barrier. The ground was strewn with blueberry bushes, another sure sign we were in the midst of bear country.

Rick elected to head up the left slope while I chose the right. We'd make a long, slow circle around the top of the ridges, meeting where the ridges came together. Ed and Joe remained near the second spike camp to await a signal as to which of the several high basins appeared promising. Even though both were at a lower elevation, Ed and Joe were first to spot a sheep, using their binoculars. Without a spotting scope the sheep appeared to be only a small white patch of snow, until it began to move. While Ed and Joe watched, ominous rain clouds moved among the peaks and over the hanging glacier several miles away. It quickly began misting and the binoculars were not strong enough to determine whether the white spot was a ram or a ewe.

"I'm going to climb closer for a better look," Ed decided. "I'll signal you whether to come up," he told Joe.

Joe kept Ed in view for about thirty minutes. Spurning grassy inclines as too steep and slippery, Ed hauled himself up over boulders and jagged rocks, skirting perpendicular granite outcroppings. Then he rounded a cliff and disappeared.

Fifteen minutes later, Joe saw Ed racing back down the hill. Instead of climbing down over the rocks, Ed was sliding down the grassy, slippery slopes on the seat of his pants. Once he fell, rolling several times and dropping his rifle, the wind knocked out of him. Only seconds later he sat up, grabbed up his rifle, and continued his mad dash down the mountain to where Joe was waiting.

"I found the grizzly!" Ed gasped. "Biggest bear I ever saw! I pulled up over a ledge and he was right there. Stood on his hind feet and roared at me! Ten feet away! He's at least nine feet tall!"

Apparently, as Ed climbed up and onto a ledge, it was already occupied. When Ed's head suddenly appeared coming over the ledge, it was a toss-up who was more surprised, Ed or the bear. Confronted with several hundred pounds of roaring fury, Ed pushed himself back off the ledge and fell seven or eight feet. He had the presence of mind to hang on to his rifle and aimed it up at the bear in case it decided to follow him down the mountain. The bear paced the ledge, however, and growled and snorted down at Ed but did not pursue. Ed speculated the bear might have been the one with the cubs we had seen earlier and so he did not shoot. But after rapidly descending the hill, Ed and Joe watched the bear on the ledge with binoculars for some time.

While all of this adventure was taking place, I was trudging farther and farther up the mountain. Just when I thought I had reached the crest, I found that the mountain didn't end where I had thought but soared several thousand feet higher. Even worse, near the actual top were some vertical rock faces where sheep gamboled happily, totally inaccessible to any hunter without ropes and pitons. Gazing skyward, I realized that the sheep were in terrain where I had no interest in going.

Several hours later, I met up with the rest of the guys at the third camp. By this time the mist had turned to hard rain and a decision had to be made to stay there and hunt several more days, or start down the mountain. Although we had our little gasoline stoves, there was no wood for a campfire. As might be expected from a guide, Rick didn't want to leave. Instead, he hoped to ensure each of us had a chance for a shot at a trophy ram.

I had worked too hard to gain that elevation and, like Rick, I wasn't keen to give it up and go back down without a shot. But as the rain continued, I noticed the water level in the creek was rising higher and higher. We had crossed that creek a number of times coming up the canyon, and I realized if the water rose too much we might not be able to cross it going back down. That would mean we would have been marooned, cut off from both our spike camp and our base camp. Reluctantly, we voted to exercise good judgement and descend the canyon before the water got any higher. We packed up and started back down the canyon about 4 PM.

Three hours later, we came to the place where we had crossed some thirty-six hours earlier. Then the water had been knee-deep and bubbling. Now it was hip-high and roaring.

(Left to right) Rick Burnham, Ed Reasor, Wayne Ross and Judge Joseph Brewer at the third camp, Little Lake Clark, Alaska (circa 1975).

Long-legged Rick started inching his way across, carrying his rifle and backpack. He almost made it. Nearing the rocky shallows on the opposite side, and only a scant twenty-five feet from where we were also waiting to cross, Rick slipped and fell into the torrent, losing his rifle. Rebounding quickly, Rick slipped off his pack, tossed it on the bank, and plunged back into the water to retrieve his Sako. Miraculously, he found it.

Then I tried it. Slowly. Carefully. With my heavy pack, I realized that the current was too swift. "Throw me a rope," I yelled to Rick.

With Joe on one end of the rope on my side of the torrent, and Rick on the far side holding his end of the rope, I slowly slid my feet along the rocky bottom and emerged from the water next to Rick.

Then it was Joe's turn, with Ed and Rick holding the rope. Four feet into the water, the current swept Joe off his feet! Down he went into the cold water, up to his neck, pack and all. Joe never let go of the rope, however. He was swung around so that he faced upstream, the water coming just below his nose and making a big rooster tail as it hit and swirled over his pack.

Ed was not wearing gloves. We could see blood spurting from his hands as the increased pressure of the rope with Joe on it started to cut into them. Ed faced several choices. He could continue to hold on, while the rope sawed into his fingers or pulled him into the water. Or he could let go of the rope leaving Joe to his own devices. Neither of the choices was pleasant.

Ed chose to hang on to the rope. "Stand up! Stand up!" he yelled at the top of his voice.

Joe, himself, was all but drained of strength and will. He realized he would be swept away if he could not regain his footing. "I prayed 'Oh God! Help!'" Joe told us that night.

Slowly, uncertainly, Joe managed to stand up. Water poured from his backpack. His rifle, camera, and binoculars were still slung around his neck and shoulders. Gradually Joe braced one foot against a rock and moved forward. One step, then another, and another, finally falling exhausted into the shallows between Rick and me.

The worst was yet to come. The rain had increased and wind howled down from the nearby peaks. We were all soaked and getting cold. And Ed was still on the other side of the creek! No one called it a creek any longer, however. As Joe wrote later: "It was a mad, rampaging river. Unable to vent its fury on rocks and boulders, it struck at anyone and anything unreasonable enough to defy its might."

The problem was how to get Ed across to our side of the canyon, now that the danger and risk had been made abundantly clear. There was now no one on Ed's side to hold the rope for him. Anchoring the rope to a tree was impossible-there were no trees. Ed realized the danger he faced.

With hand signals, we pointed out a protruding rock on which Ed had braced his feet. If Ed could tie his end of the rope onto that rock, we could hold the other end while he made his way across. To tie the rope on his side, Ed needed more slack and just as we let go of our side to give him slack, he let go of his end of the rope. Astonished, he on one side and we on the other watched as our lifeline immediately disappeared downstream!

Ed then chose to go downstream on his side of the canyon, hoping to find a better place to cross near the first spike camp. The rest of us reluctantly resumed our downward journey. We moved slowly, limping a bit now and then because of blisters on the feet and bruised and battered ankles. Now and then we glimpsed Ed across the white water, skirting boulders, climbing up and over hogbacks, and dodging in and out of the now thickening alders, just as we were forced to do.

The rain continued. We reached the second camp about 9:30 PM in the overcast, darkening twilight.

By this time Joe was almost hypothermic and shivering uncontrollably so we made him get into one of the tents and remove his sodden clothing. We quickly got a small fire going from dry wood we had stashed previously. With Joe out of the wind and rain, the next order of business was getting Ed over to the camp on our side of the canyon.

Two hundred yards upstream seemed to be the most likely place for a crossing attempt. We had found a second rope at our spike camp. Although it was longer than the one we had lost in the river, the second rope did not appear to be as strong as the first one and I expressed my concerns about it. Despite my warning, Ed, who could see the warm fire just across from where he stood, insisted he was coming to our side "now." We held on to our end of the rope while Ed tied his end around his midsection. He was then going to enter the water and, if we held on tightly, the current would swing him to our side as he floated downstream. At least that was the plan. I didn't like it but Ed was insistent.

Ed checked the rope around his waist. We grimly made sure we had a death-grip on our end. Gingerly, Ed stepped into the boiling current. As the water deepened, he let the current move him in an arc down and across the stream, deftly moving over and around boulders, feet now and then touching bottom, while striving to keep his backpack and rifle high and dry. My concerns seemed misplaced.

Then, without warning, four feet from Rick's outstretched hand, the rope broke with a sharp crack!

Ed went under the surface. He dropped his rifle. Swept downstream at an incredible rate, his first thought was that the pack would drag him under and he would drown. He thought of being knocked unconscious on the rocks. Somehow he shrugged off the pack.

When the rope broke, I saw Ed disappear. I started running downstream after him. I was passed by Rick like I was standing still.

Hearing the shouts, Joe burst out of the tent, wearing one dry sweater over his shoulders and chest, with a second one pulled over his legs, replacing his wet Levis. He saw the backpack hurtling past, then Ed's feet, then an arm. Rick came running along the shore, leaping waist-high rocks, inconceivably gaining on Ed's body being tumbled along in the current. I was right behind Rick.

Somehow, Ed found the strength to kick out, hard. He grabbed at every rock he swept by, trying to reach shallow water. The rocks tore his fingers but didn't slow him down. Finally Ed managed to hang on to a rock with the bleeding fingers of one hand. Rick reached him and grabbed Ed by the hair, and I grabbed Ed's arm. "Don't let me go, boys! I'm a hurt puppy!" Ed muttered.

Slowly we got Ed out of the whitewater. We helped him slowly to his feet, testing for broken bones. None of us knew how badly Ed might have been hurt as we examined him in the near darkness. He was battered, bruised, and bleeding and we found out later Ed had suffered two cracked ribs and a fractured hand.

Ed was quite relieved at being on solid ground and in front of a warming fire, and we were relieved to have him there. Always the wit, Ed managed to growl out "Top that, boys! Now bring on the damned bear!"

His comments lightened all of our spirits. We knew Ed would survive because no one could be dying and still maintain a sense of humor like that!

We cooked a late meal by firelight. Ed's sleeping bag (one I had loaned him) had disappeared downstream along with his pack, rifle, and binoculars. We made Ed crawl into the one dry sleeping bag that remained, while the rest of us wrapped ourselves in ponchos, sweaters, and other half-dried clothing we had warmed over the fire. We huddled in the rain-swept wind-blown tents, wretchedly enduring a bitter cold night.

Now I've siwashed overnight[19] on several occasions. I've even camped out, once, when it was so cold that the Seagram's Seven froze solid in its bottle! But that night in the canyon was the coldest, most miserable night I have ever experienced in my entire life. I curled up in my raincoat with my pack as a pillow. Once in a while I was able to doze for a few minutes only to be awakened by the noise of my teeth chattering together. The night seemed endless.

When daylight finally came, we packed up everything and made our way down to our main camp as rapidly as possible. We knew we had extra food there, and plenty of dry clothes to get us warm again.

---

[19] Siwash means to sleep outside, overnight, without benefit of any shelter or sleeping bag, wherever your day's end finds you.

Alas, it was not to be. When we got to the main camp at the lake, we found in our absence, we had had a visitor. Mr. Bear had paid us a visit, torn up our tent, eaten our food, and scattered our belongings.

We were most relieved to see Larry fly in that evening to pick us up. As Larry taxied up the lake prior to takeoff, I remarked that it certainly was not "a gradual walk up to the sheep" nor did we find the "nice game trail on the eastern side of the canyon" Larry had promised.

"I know!" Larry confessed. "On the way in to pick you guys up this afternoon, I realized I must have dropped you all off at the wrong canyon!"

Chapter 30
The Cordova Office

As the junior member of the firm, and even though I was a partner. I was often designated as the guy who had to "cover the Cordova office."

Cordova is a small town on Prince William Sound east of Anchorage, and it is accessible only by air or ship. In the early 1900s it was the terminus of the *Copper River and Northwest Railroad* which went from tidewater to the Kennecott copper mines, located in one of the largest copper deposits in the world. The mine closed in the late 1930s and the railroad tracks were torn up shortly thereafter. For the last half century, the primary industry in Cordova has been commercial fishing.

Originally, our Cordova office was in a small A-frame about six blocks from downtown. In those days it cost only forty or fifty bucks to fly round trip to Cordova. At that rate we could afford to send someone down to Cordova every week. When it was my turn I'd fly down early on Friday, attend court, meet with clients, and fly back around seven in the evening. When the salmon were in the Eyak River, or the ducks were flying, however, I'd stay until Saturday. Our part-time secretary lived in the A-frame with her husband and kids. So when I stayed overnight, I had to stay in a hotel.

At the time we represented a fellow who owned one of the oldest hotels in Cordova. Evidently he liked us because he always gave us one of the "deluxe" rooms on the second floor. The deluxe rooms were different from most of the other rooms. The deluxe rooms had a window and a sink. The window overlooked Main Street. The bathroom was down the hall.

On the first floor of the hotel was the wildest bar in Cordova. It featured a guy called the "One-Man Band." He strummed a guitar while singing and playing the harmonica. At the same time, he had an electronic bass that went *boom boom boom da boom, boom boom boom da boom* incessantly.

The One-Man Band had a favorite song, "The Yellow Rose of Texas," which he played quite often. When he was drinking, which was every night, he'd often forget he had just finished singing "The Yellow Rose of Texas" and he'd sing it again. In fact, just about every other song he sang was "The Yellow Rose of Texas," and that went on all night, until around 2:00 AM. Of course, the "One-Man Band" had the volume on his microphone turned up full blast, and his electronic bass was *boom boom boom da booming* full volume as well.

The deluxe room we were given by our client, the hotel owner, was located directly over the bandstand. As a result, when the One-Man Band started up, generally around 10:00 PM, the entire deluxe room vibrated violently, in a *boom boom boom da boom* cadence, while the sounds of a guitar, a harmonica and "The Yellow Rose of Texas" blasted through the thin wood floor. This, of course, made sleeping a real challenge.

In the wintertime, the drain in the sink in the deluxe room would freeze. Unfortunately, the faucet flowing into the sink didn't. It dripped instead. It dripped very loudly-*ploop, ploop, ploop.*

Of course, when the water dripped into the sink because the drain was frozen, the water had no other option but to fill up the sink. It did this quite quickly.

When the sink filled up, the water leaked over the side of the sink-*plop, plop, plop.* To keep the room from flooding, we had to put a waste-basket under the sink to catch the water dripping out of the sink.

Thus, in addition to the sounds of a guitar, a harmonica, an electronic bass going *boom boom boom da boom*, and "The Yellow Rose of Texas" for the umpteenth time, we endured the *ploop-plop, ploop-plop, ploop-plop* of dripping water within six feet of our beds.

Generally around 1:00 AM the *ploop-plop, ploop-plop* took on a new urgency, and we'd recognize from the sound that the wastebasket had filled with water and needed emptying. When that happened, of course, we were faced with a problem: Where does one get rid of five or so gallons of water when the drains are frozen?

The answer, of course, was simple. After all, we had the deluxe room with a window that overlooked Main Street.

Whenever the wastebasket needed emptying, we merely lugged it to our window, raised the sash and poured the full bucket of water out the window. Occasionally a bar patron picked just that moment to walk out of the front door of the bar, and found himself doused with a deluge of water. Generally, however, the water merely hit the sidewalk where it promptly froze.

Often bar patrons came out of the bar, slid on the ice, and fell down. Nobody ever got hurt, mainly, I think, because at that hour of the morning none of them was capable of feeling any pain. Or if they did get hurt, we never got hired as attorneys to sue on their behalf. That was probably a good thing. After all, it would have been somewhat embarrassing to represent someone suing our own landlord for a slip and fall case when we had caused the accident!

I remember one time the fire marshal closed down our client's hotel as a fire hazard and wouldn't let the owner reopen the hotel until fire escapes were installed. Our client dutifully installed fire escapes constructed out of 2-by-4s, and was allowed to reopen. We always felt, however, if there ever had been a fire, the first thing to burn would have been those 2-by-4s.

In the summertime we also worried about a fire in the hotel when we stayed there. We'd always greet the morning with a prayer of thanksgiving for having survived the night. In the winter, however, we didn't worry about fires. After all, we always had a wastebasket full of water in our room!

———

Eventually, we bought a house trailer for an office. It was located in the Vina Young Subdivision and since it had several bedrooms, we didn't have to stay in that hotel anymore.

If it was my weekend for the Cordova office duty and I stayed overnight in the trailer office, I'd often trudge down to Davis Super Foods and buy a nice big steak. Perry Davis sold the best meat in Alaska. I then returned to the office and cooked it over the office charcoal grill, and ate a fine meal liberally washed down with some adult libation. The office had a supply of good books and magazines to read and I often spent a quiet, comfortable evening away from the bustle of Anchorage.

———

Once in a while I went downtown and had a drink at one or two of the local Cordova watering holes. I remember walking downtown one evening and passing the Catholic Church and rectory. I had heard there was a priest from Anchorage visiting in town. So my conscience took over. Here was a priest, I thought, sitting all alone in the rectory, in a strange town on a Saturday night. Perhaps I should stop in, introduce myself, and visit with him for a while? Certainly that would be better for my soul than getting a drink at one of the local bars? So I walked up to the door and knocked. Father Powers came to the door and I introduced myself.

"Hi, Father! I wanted to introduce myself. I'm Wayne Ross and I go to Saint Elizabeth Seaton Church in Anchorage," I said.

"So?" said Father Powers. Then he walked back into the rectory and closed the door.

And I resumed my walk downtown to get a drink, with a clear conscience.

I found out later Father Powers was not known as "Father Warmth."

————

In the late '70s and early '80s Cordova was a bustling town. Several lawyers lived and maintained their offices there full time. A few lawyers came in from Valdez from time to time. And then there were my partners and I who flew down from Anchorage. The district attorney's office in Anchorage also assigned an assistant DA part-time to Cordova.

The old Cordova Courthouse was located above the post office. The courtroom had a magnificent view of the harbor and looked just like the courtrooms seen in old western movies. It was always a treat to try cases there. Magistrate Mary Wentworth was a very pretty lady, with a personality to match. Unlike Father Powers, she always made us welcome when we came to Cordova. In fact, we made it a point to stop in and see her when one of us was in town.

And Cordova cases were often a lot of fun.

————

One such fun case involved a young man charged with driving while his driver's license was suspended. The defendant claimed the police officer had mistaken him for his brother, who was really driving the car. The brother backed up the story.

A jury was empaneled and the DA called the citing officer to the stand. The officer testified he had seen my client driving down Main Street and watched him turn the corner. The officer knew my client's license had been suspended, so he hot-footed it down the street and around the corner. There he found my client sitting in the passenger's seat of the parked car with the keys in the ignition.

"My brother was driving!" protested my client. "He's in the grocery store!" The officer ignored the young man's explanation and took him off to jail.

When I got to cross-examine at trial, I asked the officer to draw a map on the blackboard showing where he was when he first saw my client, the corner, and the location where the arrest took place. The officer complied. I then asked the officer to indicate directions. The officer drew an N for north on the top of the map, and an S for south on the bottom of the map. He then drew a W for west on the right side of the map, and an E for east on the left side of the map. The jury snickered. It was obvious the officer had his directions confused.

I asked the officer if the sun could have been in his eyes at the time of his claimed sighting of my client, since the time was late afternoon. The officer said he didn't believe the setting sun interfered with his view. I then asked the officer to indicate on the map where the sun was at the time he allegedly saw my client. He hesitated, and I asked him if he understood the request.

"I do," said the policeman, "but I can't remember whether the sun comes up in the east and goes down in the west, or if it comes up in the west and goes down in the east?"

In my final argument, of course, I reminded the jury that the arresting officer was less than a credible witness. "He doesn't even know which direction the sun comes up!" The jury was out ten minutes and acquitted my client.

―――――

Another case, less fun, found me defending a fellow charged with first-degree murder. He had shot another man, less than seventy-five feet from the police station and in front of a witness, over the affections of a woman. Because the defendant had been heavily intoxicated at the time, I hoped I could get the jury to reject the first-degree-murder charge and settle on manslaughter, a lesser charge.

I tried, unsuccessfully, to get my client to allow me to change the place of trial to Anchorage. "I want to go to trial in Cordova!" my client explained. "I drink with everybody in town. They are all my friends! I'm not worried."

So I was stuck with trying the case in Cordova where everyone knew either my client or the deceased, or often both.

I lined up the local alcohol counselor as an expert witness on alcoholism. He gave my client some funky test and was prepared to testify that my client was an alcoholic; and if he was drinking, as he usually was, he probably could not have formed the necessary intent to kill to justify a first-degree-murder conviction.

The morning of trial I told the DA the names of my witnesses, including the name of our expert witness, the alcohol counselor. Under the criminal rules, I should have revealed the name of our expert long before, but I had discovered there was an alcoholic counselor in Cordova only the day before trial. And I had gotten the guy to be my expert only the night before trial. So, of course, I could tell the DA about my expert only on the day of trial.

Several hours later during a recess in the trial, the DA, Bill Cook[20], advised me my expert witness was a bank robber from Hawaii and Bill was prepared to reveal that fact to the jury. When I spoke to my expert, he admitted he was, indeed, a bank robber from Hawaii, but claimed he had "reformed." He certainly didn't want the local citizens to know about his past, however, so my expert now refused to testify.

Now without an expert, I nevertheless argued for a verdict of man-slaughter rather than one of first-degree-murder. I stated it was impossible for my client to have formed the intent to kill necessary for a murder charge because he was obviously drunk. I proved my client had been in the bar all afternoon and had consumed more than twenty mixed drinks. I proved that he was thinking of other things besides murder shortly before the killing. My witness was one of the local "sporting women" who testified that only twenty minutes before the killing my client had propositioned her. My client claimed that after being turned down by this woman, he decided to go talk to his former girlfriend to attempt reconciliation. I argued that my client had taken his rifle "only for self-defense" from her new boyfriend. I showed that my client had loaded only one bullet into the rifle. "Someone intent on murder would have loaded his gun with all the bullets it would take!" I argued. I pointed out that the killing took place only seventy-five feet from the Cordova police station. "Nobody who planned a murder would do it only seventy-five feet from a police station!" I reasoned to the jury. I even discovered and proved the decedent had a knife on his person when he was killed and the police, instead of seizing the knife as evidence, had given the knife away. And in fact, the police had not even noted, much less remembered, just how big that knife was!

While the jury was deliberating, my client told me I had done "a great job"!

After the jury rendered its verdict of first-degree-murder, my investigator, Steve Richards, told me I was lucky in losing. "The decedent's brother was sitting behind you with a loaded nine millimeter pistol under his coat!" Steve said. "He said he intended to kill our client, and you, if you got the guy off!"

"Why didn't you warn me?" I asked incredulously.

"I didn't want to put a crimp in your style," said Steve with a grin. "Besides," Steve added, "I had him covered with my forty-five!"

---

[20] Later Bill Cook worked as an associate attorney in my office.

That evening I visited one of the local bars. The jury was there and the jury foreman insisted on buying me a drink. "Good job in arguing for manslaughter," he said, "but, remember, we drank with your client for years. We knew he was a bum, and so we voted to just find him guilty of whatever charge would put him in jail the longest."

With friends like Steve Richards, and my client's drinking buddies on the jury, who needs enemies?

———

We had a dear little lady in Cordova who, somehow, "adopted" us. Her name was Vina Young. She wasn't young however. Instead, she was old. Very old! Indeed, Vina claimed she didn't know herself how old she really was. She said she had two birth certificates. One said she was born in 1888 and the other said 1893. She didn't know which one was right.

We called Vina "Our Gal Friday."

We'd call Vina from Anchorage and tell her when we would be flying into Cordova. Vina always met our plane. Then she drove us the thirteen miles into town in her old pickup, filling us in on the latest Cordova happenings. We'd learn who had been arrested, who was sleeping with whom, and every other piece of gossip she had heard since last we came. Vina loved to drive us around and she called us "her boys."

The truck she drove when we first had our office in Cordova was an old Chevrolet step-side pickup. She liked the truck but complained that "they don't make batteries anymore like they used to!" She said her previous truck had a much better battery than her present one. She claimed she had gone twenty-three years on a battery in her first truck but "I only got twelve years of service on this one!" She thought the first battery had lasted so long because she always filled it with spring water."Now I am getting too old to haul spring water. Maybe that is why the newer battery didn't last me twenty-three years."

Vina had been born in Minnesota and had lived on a remote farm there. Eventually she married a man who "had a hankering for Alaska and who thought it was possible to ride a train to the Fairbanks goldfields from Cordova." She and her husband arrived in Cordova in July 1934, when the copper mines and railroad were in full operation. In later years Vina referred to her former husband as a "squaw man." She said the marriage didn't work out "because he was always chasing local women." Finally, Vina divorced him.

Allegedly, on her first day in Cordova Vina was given the chance to buy a cow, and eventually established the first dairy in the area. She said she furnished fresh milk to the copper miners in Kennecott. "I supplied all the milk to the workers at the Kennecott mines!" she'd say proudly.

One day the workers, to show their appreciation, scheduled a birthday party for Vina at one of the mines and they arranged for her to ride the Copper River and Northwestern Railroad from Cordova to Kennecott. She told how they seated her on the open rear platform of the last car, bundled her up with blankets, and how she rode "up the line" enjoying the beautiful scenery.

When Vina got to Kennecott, however, she found out she would have to ride in an ore bucket on an aerial tramway several hundred feet in the air to get to where the party was.

"They had the party without me!" Vina explained. "There was no way they were going to get me into that bucket!"

Over the years, Vina operated the town's telephone switchboard and then opened a trailer court. Eventually it was one of her trailers that we bought to use for our Cordova office.

One of Vina's most prized possessions was a Deluxe Winchester Model 64 in .30-30. She had purchased it the day the Japanese attacked Dutch Harbor, Alaska. She told how she bought the gun at the Cordova hardware store along with ten boxes of ammunition. She then set up a firing position in one of the ventilators on the roof of her cow barn. She supplied it with several large bottles of water and boxes of pilot bread. "I could see a long ways from there," Vina explained. "I figured when the Japs attacked Cordova they might get me eventually, but I'd get plenty of them first!"

Whenever I went on a hike, or fishing, Vina insisted that I carry her .30-30. "There are a lot of bears around here," she'd say. "You'd better take a big gun with you! Take my .30-30."

And I always did.

One time a large brown bear started coming up onto Vina's porch at night to try and get her little dog. Vina complained to the Fish & Game people and she said she'd shoot the bear "if it hurts my little dog." Vina had to be in her nineties at the time and the local Fish & Game officer called me and asked me to have a talk with her. He explained he had threatened to arrest Vina if she shot the bear. "We are afraid she'll get hurt or killed if she goes after that bear!" the officer stated.

"She's killed three brownies already with her rifle!" I responded. "If I were you I'd worry more about the bear then I would about Vina!"

Later I took Vina aside and told her if she had to shoot the bear in defense of herself or her dog she should not call the Fish & Game about it. Instead she should call me first. I told her that I would report the dead bear to Fish & Game. "And I'll tell them the bear committed suicide on your front porch!"

In 1977 Vina decided to buy a new truck. I had a friend in the business and arranged to have him send her a Chevrolet truck catalog. After going through the catalog, she found a picture of the exact truck she wanted. She purchased a brand-new Chevy pickup, another step-side, black with red and blue pinstriping, mag wheels, and a big V-8. Every kid in Cordova was envious of Vina's new truck.

After a while Vina began to become forgetful. Finally, after a fire at her house, it became obvious she needed to be in extended care. A relative of hers came up from Minnesota to pick her up and take care of her back there. Several years later, we got word Vina had died. Her listed age was 101.

I still have her .30-30.

————

Cordova had more than its share of interesting people. One guy I always enjoyed was Frank. Frank was a part-time gunsmith and worked full-time at the Cordova airport. Often when he knew I was in town overnight, he'd stop in at our office and we'd swap stories and, occasionally, even guns.

One year Frank decided he was going to collect swords. He had one or two of what I would call "plain vanilla" swords of no particular rarity or value.

That same year some Cordova civic organization decided it was going to have a gun show. I flew down there and rented a table. Frank had to work at the airport part of the day so he could not be at the show full-time. He put a pair of very nice original Mauser rifles for sale on a table he had rented and he told me what he wanted for each. Frank asked me to watch his table while he was at work.

Several hours later a fellow came in and inquired about the Mausers. I told him what I knew and he wanted to know if the owner might be interested in doing some trading. I told the guy Frank was interested in swords and the guy could talk to Frank by driving out to the airport.

The guy came back in another hour with a note from Frank. The note told me I should give the man the two Mauser rifles. It said Frank had given the guy the rifles in trade for a sword, and Frank would stop in at my office that evening to show it to me.

Frank showed up about at 8:00 PM with a big grin on his face. He said he had traded for a rare antique Spanish sword with a genuine Toledo steel blade. According to Frank, the sword even had the owner's initials, K.P., in fancy filigree on the scabbard. Frank pulled his new precious sword out to show me.

I looked it over and had to give Frank the bad news. "K.P." stood for *Knights of Pythias*, a fraternal group, and were not the initials of some Spanish nobleman. The marking on the blade didn't refer to Toledo steel. Instead, it said "Cincinnati Ornament Co., Toledo, Ohio." I hated to tell Frank his two Mausers had been worth five times what the sword was.

That night Frank gave up the idea of collecting swords and went back to collecting guns.

———

While we had our Cordova office, we became friends with Tom. Tom and his wife lived outside of town and their cabin was accessible only by boat. Tom had a fishing boat and on one occasion he took me on a hunting trip. We cruised all of the way around Hinchinbrook Island, anchoring up in Constantine Harbor one night. In the evenings we played poker and drank adult beverages. It was a great trip.

On another occasion Ed Reasor and my dad accompanied us on a cruise with Tom. We were hunting for geese and Reasor, Tom, and I each had shotguns. We saw no geese but, on one day, we saw eighteen black bears. We decided to take one or two of those bear. Our shotguns were no good for bear but Tom had an old Model 70 Winchester aboard his boat. The Winchester was in .22 Hornet, a varmint cartridge. Tom called the rifle his "seal gun" because he used it to shoot seals when they got tangled in his fishing nets before the seals could destroy the nets. The seal Gun wasn't really a bear gun either, but it was all that we had.

We anchored up in Sheep Bay and rowed ashore. Reasor and I had our shotguns and Tom had the Hornet. He killed the first black bear we saw with one shot at about 175 yards. The bear dropped at the shot and never moved a muscle. While Reasor and I skinned the bear, another bear came running past us at about forty yards. I was carrying a two-inch-barreled Colt New Service revolver in .45 Colt and emptied the gun at the running bear. I succeeded only in making the bear run faster.

Later that day we got a second black bear with the Hornet at a measured 325 yards, again with only one shot. When hit, the bear ran only about thirty yards before collapsing.

On the way back to Tom's cabin, we pulled into another small bay, still looking for geese, and saw a buoy marking where a crab pot had been baited and set. Tom called whoever set the pot a "Sooner" because the crabbing season did not open until the next day. We pulled the crab pot up and there were a half dozen Dungeness crabs. "We've got dinner!"

Tom announced. He then put a six-pack of beer into the crab pot before resubmerging it so when the Sooner eventually pulled up his illegal crab pot he would know someone had been wise to him.

Later, at Tom's cabin, my father boiled the crab for dinner. Dad loved crab, especially when it was cooked in caraway seed, and that was just the way it was done that night. Dad remarked he thought he was in heaven. "I've never been anywhere before where I could eat crab until I had no room for more!" he said.

After dinner, the cards and libation were brought out and we played poker until about one in the morning. Tom's wife joined the game and shared the libation. After the game, we all went to sleep (Reasor and I on the floor in sleeping bags). About 2:00 AM, Tom's wife started hollering. "Tom! Tom! I can't find the bedroom! Help me Tom!" We then could hear her banging around in the other room of the cabin. Reasor and I both burrowed deeper in our sleeping bags. It was obvious Tom's wife had far too much to drink that night and we deemed it best to not get involved.

Nonetheless, at 6:00 AM, we heard noise in the kitchen. Tom's wife was in there busily making breakfast, seemingly none the worse for wear. She was singing and totally pleasant. She showed no sign of a hangover, and no remembrance of the occurrences of the night before. That gal could drink!

Later Tom and his wife sold the cabin and moved to the Lower 48. I offered to buy the Hornet but Tom wouldn't part with it. Every Christmas I'd write them, asking how the Hornet was. He'd write back "The Hornet is fine!" After Tom died, I wrote his wife and again asked to buy the Hornet, but Tom's son wanted it and so it wasn't for sale.

I still wish I could have bought it.

————

Eventually we sold our trailer office in Cordova, and Barbara and I then bought a good-sized building on Main Street across from the Masonic Hall. Cordova had more snow and rain than Anchorage and it was fun to go there in the winter and spend a quiet evening in the office, reading and watching the snow and rain come down.

Over the years however, the Anchorage-Cordova round-trip airfare doubled, then doubled again, and it became more and more expensive and thus difficult to justify maintaining an office there. Spending hundreds of dollars for an overnight trip to Cordova, when clients might or might not be waiting, didn't make much sense. We could simply stay in Anchorage, where we were assured of business every day.

Furthermore, I noticed my Cordova began to change. The town seemed evenly divided between those who wanted a highway to be built connecting Cordova to the rest of Alaska, and those who opposed the road. Without the town's backing, the road never materialized. A philosopher said "You either grow or die." Cordova began dying. A number of businesses closed. Davis's Super Foods ceased to exist. The other attorneys moved on to other towns. Kids moved elsewhere where jobs were more available. Older citizens died. The big hotel, The Reluctant Fisherman, closed its doors. There were more and more vacant store windows on Main Street.

Many Cordovans didn't seem to notice or care. They were living in one of the most beautiful towns in Alaska, and that was good enough for them. Unfortunately, it wasn't good enough for me. I had a wife and kids to feed, and Cordova wasn't helping me do that. Cases became fewer and sometimes when they did arise, the clients didn't bother to keep current on their attorney fees. Even so-called friends failed to keep their commitments to my office. Frank's daughter, for example, stiffed my office for more than $8,000 after we successfully helped her to get a divorce and custody of her children.

Finally, we sold our building on Main Street, and closed our Cordova office. It was no longer financially justifiable to keep going there.

Several years ago I went to Cordova on political business. Seeing Cordova on that occasion was quite disappointing-almost like, after many years seeing a girl whom you had once loved and discovering that she had gone to seed. Even though the scenic beauty of the area was still there, the vitality of the town had vanished. It had grown old and tawdry. I felt a sense of loss and sadness for what once had been.

Chapter 31
The Weiss Adler

I first met the Weiss Adler in the mid-'70s. A fellow attorney, Bob Griffin, had arranged a caribou hunt out on the Alaskan Peninsula, and asked me to go along. The Weiss Adler was to be the pilot.

It was March and it was cold. We had flown out toward "Bet-yur-ass-off" Lake on the Alaska Peninsula and, after locating some caribou herds from the air, we discovered an abandoned cabin which looked like a good place to spend the night.

The Weiss Adler was flying a Cessna 182 on wheels and when he came in for a landing on the ice-covered lake, we found the brakes of the plane were virtually useless for stopping on the icy surface. We slid and slid, much farther than we thought we would. Finally, we saw we were sliding toward an open lead in the ice and were in danger of dropping into the lake. The Weiss Adler gunned the engine and, at the last moment, lifted the plane off the surface of the lake and over the open lead. I realized then he was a very good pilot.

Later that evening as we were getting settled in the old cabin, the wind started to pick up. My impressions of the Weiss Adler's piloting skills were reinforced when he elected to spend the night in the airplane. "With a wind like this, you never know what might happen to a plane sitting out on the ice," he said.

Around 3:00 AM Bob and I were awakened by the sounds of three shots, the signal for distress. Throwing on our clothes, we stumbled out of the shack into the stormy night. Again we heard three shots. They came from the lake and we headed in that direction. When we got to the shore, we noticed a lead of dark windswept water had opened up between the shore and the airplane. We were cut off from the plane! The ice of the lake was threatening to break up.

The Weiss Adler had fired the shots. He now stood beside his airplane, cut off from us and the shore. "I'll be back for you!" he shouted. He then climbed into the plane and started it up. The last we saw of the Weiss Adler and the plane was its lights as it taxied away from us across the lake, skirting the open leads and looking for enough solid ice to survive the night.

There wasn't anything we on the shore could do to help, so we went back to the cabin. At daybreak we arose and went down to the lake. We saw that the Weiss Adler and the plane had made it through the night far out on the lake. We also saw we were still separated from the plane by about thirty yards of open water. Shortly thereafter, we heard the rumble of the airplane's engine and saw it take off from the ice, heading toward us. As the plane flew over, a roll of toilet paper came sailing down out of its window. We walked to where it had fallen and picked up the roll. On it was written: "Thought you could use this. Good luck in getting a caribou. I'll be back tomorrow morning."

We did get a caribou that day and the Weiss Adler did come back the next. He had flown to King Salmon and had searched there all day for a rubber raft. Apparently, rubber rafts are not readily available in King Salmon in March, but find one he did, and the next morning saw us ferrying caribou meat and ourselves from the shore, across the open lead, to the pan of ice on which the plane sat. And aside from some scary moments when the lead closed up while we were trying to cross it in the raft, threatening to smash us between pans of ice weighing thousands of tons, we did make it home safely.

The Weiss Adler wasn't always known as the Weiss Adler. Before he got that name he had been known as Gerald Yeiter, and he had been a trespass investigator for the BLM. Yeiter got the name the "Weiss Adler" (the White Eagle) from a German hunter, who had come to Alaska to hunt caribou and to fish near Ugashik Lake on the Alaskan Peninsula west of Anchorage.

That year the Weiss Adler had been guiding a group of German hunters, and I was along as an assistant guide. One German (I'll call him Rudi) flew into the Weiss Adler's Ugashik Camp and was unhappy to find there were no hot showers. An overly fastidious fellow, Rudi wasn't pleased with the rustic accommodations and wanted to go back to town as soon as possible. As a result, as soon as he could, Rudi shot a little bitty caribou the first day of hunting and then announced he wanted to return to King Salmon immediately. He made such a fuss about it the Weiss Adler agreed to fly Rudi there. The Weiss Adler asked me to go along and I got into the copilot's seat.

After we took off, the Weiss Adler radioed King Salmon for a weather report. He was told the wind was gusting to sixty-five miles per hour and, as a result, the Weiss Adler announced we could not go to King Salmon because of weather … we would have to return to camp.

Rudi went nuts. He started yelling he wanted to go to King Salmon. He *insisted* we go to King Salmon! When the Weiss Adler again told Rudi it was too dangerous to land in King Salmon because of the wind, and we were returning to camp, Rudi started beating the Weiss Adler about the head. The plane began bouncing all over the sky as the Weiss Adler tried to maintain control of the aircraft while warding off punches from Rudi, who was in the back seat. "Shoot that son-of- a-bitch!" the Weiss Adler shouted at me. "He's going to wreck the plane!"

I pulled out my .45 revolver and pointed it back at Rudi, who immediately calmed down. When we landed back at camp, Rudi got out of the plane. "I vill get chu for thizzz!" he hissed at me. "I am a member of the Lionzzzz Club, und I zaw dey have a Lionzzzz Club in King Zalmon. Venn ve get to King Salmon, I vill report chu to the Lionzzzz Club! Denn chu will be zorry!"

Later that day the Weiss Adler tried again to get Rudi out of camp and back to King Salmon. The Weiss Adler again asked me to ride shotgun. This time we made it to King Salmon, and once on the ground, Rudi broke into a big smile. He was once again back in civilization and he was happy because he could now get a hot shower. Rudi even treated the Weiss Adler and me to a big steak dinner at Eddie's Fireside Lounge.

I never did hear from the Lion's Club.

———

On another occasion, we were weathered in at a cabin along the Naknek River on the Alaska Peninsula. The wind howled outside as I cut the pasteboards for it seemed the hundredth time. Three-handed poker was becoming tedious, not only to me but to my companions, attorney Bob Griffin and the Weiss Adler. We had been weathered in for two days and it almost looked as if we'd never get out to hunt caribou.

"When do you think we'll be able to get out and hunt?" I asked the Weiss Adler.

Just then the Weiss Adler spied a movement along the floor near the Avon inflatable raft that was stored in the cabin.

"How about now?" the Weiss Adler answered. "I'll take you on a hunt right now and guarantee you a shot but it's going to cost you."

"Right now I'd pay anything just to go hunting!" I answered.

"The price is $1,000," said the Weiss Adler, "and you will have a shot at a trophy mouse. Price includes cleaning and mounting."

"Alright," I said, unloading the jacketed bullets from the .45 caliber Colt New Service revolver lying on the table. I then reloaded a chamber with one of my special birdshot reloads so-I thought-when I next cocked the hammer the chamber containing the birdshot would rotate under the hammer.

"Are you ready?" the Weiss Adler asked.

"Ready," I answered, cocking the revolver.

The Weiss Adler jumped onto the Avon raft. Out of the raft came a trophy bull mouse. The mouse ran down the rope of the raft to the floor. Halfway across the floor to the door he paused. I took careful aim, trying to determine the best place to nail him. I pulled the trigger.

Instead of the anticipated roar of the Colt I was greeted with a hollow "click." The trophy bull mouse stuck his tongue out at me and ran through the crack in the door.

"What happened?" the Weiss Adler asked. His question could barely be heard above the jeers and catcalls of Bob Griffin.

At first I didn't know and then I examined the Colt. I had forgotten Colt revolvers rotate to the right. I usually carry a Smith & Wesson in .45 Long Colt and had been carrying a Smith & Wesson so long I had loaded the cartridge in on the right side of the cylinder. Which of course was the wrong side of the cylinder. I had anticipated upon cocking the revolver the cylinder would turn left bringing the cartridge under the hammer. If the revolver had been a Smith that would have happened. Smiths rotate to the left. Since the revolver was a Colt, however, upon cocking, the cartridge rotated further to the right and the hammer fell on an empty chamber. Needless to say, I took a lot of kidding the rest of the day.

Determined to redeem myself, I practiced reloading the Colt the proper way. I doubted if I would get another shot at such a trophy mouse but I wanted to be ready if the chance presented itself.

Towards evening, the trophy mouse slipped in at the crack in the door. He made it back to the Avon raft before I could even draw.

"Do you want to try again?" asked the Weiss Adler.

I allowed as I did.

"It'll cost you another $1,000."

I agreed. Anything was better than to have to put up with the bantering I had to endure from the Weiss Adler and Bob all afternoon.

"Are you ready?" the Weiss Adler asked.

I checked the revolver, cocking it to make sure the birdshot cartridge was under the hammer this time. It was. "Ready!" I answered. The adrenalin began pumping through my veins. I felt the awakening of buck fever. I sought to control myself, forcing myself to remain calm.

"Ready!" I answered again.

The Weiss Adler jumped onto the Avon raft. Out of the raft came the trophy bull mouse. He ran down the rope of the raft to the floor. Again he paused halfway across the floor to the door. I took careful aim and fired. The big Colt roared.

The birdshot canister in the cartridge, which was supposed to break up in the barrel of the gun allowing the shot to spread, stayed together. Apparently when I reloaded the cartridge, I hadn't put enough powder in it. Thus, the plastic capsule containing the birdshot hit a half inch behind the mouse tearing a big hole in the carpet. Upon hitting the floor the capsule broke up allowing the shot to escape. Shot bounced all over the room. All over, that is, except where the trophy bull mouse was standing. The mouse again stuck his tongue out at me, and nonchalantly scurried out the crack in the door.

The jeering and catcalls of the Weiss Adler and Bob are best left to your imagination, dear reader. My reputation as a hunter of big game was thoroughly soiled. I did not see the trophy mouse again that trip, but vowed I would return to the Naknek River next season for that trophy mouse.

During the intervening year the Weiss Adler and Bob never let me forget the trophy mouse. The Weiss Adler even had a cartoon drawn by a professional artist which hangs in my lodge showing me missing the trophy mouse.

The following fall I returned to the Naknek River determined to bag that wily mouse. Although I hunted for several days, no animal of his size presented itself and I was about to give up hope. Then one evening after supper, Jerry and I decided to go fishing.

Since it was cold and raining, I put my Woolrich coat on over a Smith & Wesson .45 I carried in a shoulder holster. Then I put on a raincoat. Then I put on a life jacket since we planned to fish from the boat. We stepped out onto the porch.

I caught a glimpse of movement out of the corner of my eye. The trophy bull mouse lay crouched on the porch behind a brick by my foot. I grabbed for my gun but knew I couldn't get it out from under life jacket and raincoat in time before the mouse would spring.

Apparently realizing instinctively it was only a matter of milliseconds before the bull mouse would be on me, I kicked the brick squashing the bull mouse against the wall.

I managed to get my revolver out and we approached the trophy bull mouse from the downwind side. We both were prepared to fire, should the mouse charge. Upon close examination however, we discovered I had gotten it with the first kick, or the first brick, or the first kick of the brick, and the trophy mouse was truly dead.

My hunting prowess was re-recognized from that day on.

The Weiss Adler and the author with the $1000 mouse.

The trophy bull mouse was never skinned and mounted. There were too many rub marks on its hide caused by the brick. We photographed it from all angles, however, and measured it for Boone and Crockett should they decide to open up a class for record trophy bull mice.

The Weiss Adler never sent me a bill for the hunt. I continued to do legal work for him from time to time but I didn't bill him either. Whenever-if ever-I got his bill, I'd send him mine. I'm a firm believer in the old law school maxim, "Always get the other guy's bill first!"

The Weiss Adler and I had a lot of adventures over the next few years. These included a 125 mile flight for a six-pack of Coke; landing on a river at night by the light of a Coleman lantern when a burnt fuse caused the plane's landing lights to go out; spotting, stalking, and taking a forty-two inch moose with a revolver; watching the entire countryside light up one night from what could only have been a meteor; and other adventures.

Several years passed and I didn't see the Weiss Adler much. I was saddened to learn that in early 1990, while the Weiss Adler was riding as a passenger in a plane flown by a novice pilot, Yeiter was killed when the plane's engine stalled coming in for a landing on Finger Lake.

I guess there isn't too much a fellow can leave behind him when its his time to go, except perhaps good memories in the people he affected.

The Weiss Adler left me with a lot of good memories, including some hair-raising adventures that, once they were over, I was glad I experienced. For these I will always be grateful. He is, and forever will be, missed.

Chapter 32
The Glennallen Office

The announcement about finding large quantities of oil on Alaska's North Slope resulted in the decision to build the Alaska Pipeline, running 810 miles from the Slope to tidewater in Valdez. I worked with Ed Reasor during a portion of the Pipeline Boom.

One of the towns on the intended pipeline route was Glennallen, a little town on the road system about 186 miles northeast of Anchorage. A pipeline construction camp was located in the area. Since Glennallen did not have a resident attorney, but it did have a magistrate[21], we decided we should explore the idea of locating a branch office there like we had in Cordova.

One sunny spring day the attorneys in Reasor's office drove to Glennallen to see what might be available in the way of office space to rent. Because of the boom, we found little available. One of Reasor's clients in Anchorage, however, had an 8 by 32 foot house trailer he was willing to sell. Since Glennallen sometimes had temperatures as low as sixty degrees below zero, Ed had a 55,000 BTU furnace installed in the little trailer. He also had bunk beds constructed in the back bedroom, and we then hauled the trailer to Glennallen.

We rented a space for our office trailer next to Bushy Bob McIntosh's Glennallen Lodge. We hooked up to the lodge's water and septic and opened for business. Initially, one of us would drive up from Anchorage to cover that office a day or two during the week. Shortly after we opened it, however, we hired a law clerk named Bill McNall to cover the outlying offices.

The trailer office had a little kitchen and breakfast nook in the front, a small bathroom, and the small bedroom with the bunk beds in the rear.

---

[21] My first introduction to that magistrate is contained in Chapter 26.

It was really quite comfortable in the summertime. The winter, however, was another matter entirely.

The trailer had been constructed in Florida and if it had any insulation at all, it was *de minimus*. Once the outside temperature fell below minus twenty degrees, the trailer windows iced up so much you could not see out of them.

There was a thermometer on the control panel for the 55,000 BTU furnace we had installed. If you watched, you could actually see the temperature on the thermometer drop. We'd set the heat at sixty-eight degrees and the heater would turn on with a loud thump. Shortly thereafter, when the heater was going, the inside heater fan engaged. Of course, the heater and its fan were for a much larger structure. The fan was so powerful it would lift our paperwork from the kitchen table and skitter it across the surface, and often onto the floor. In the winter we had to make sure all of our paperwork was weighted down or it would blow away.

In a minute or two, the oversized heater would heat the entire trailer. While the heater was running, we could actually see the temperature on the thermostat rise. When the heater shut off, we could watch the thermostat's temperature plummet. The entire procedure, up and down, repeated every three or four minutes.

With all the heat going on and off, the trailer became quite dry inside. Anyone who stayed in the trailer overnight in the winter often woke up with a nosebleed.

That wasn't the biggest problem, however. The biggest problem was that the water and sewer would freeze up. As a result, in the winter, we had no running water and no toilet or shower. To attend to those bodily needs, we'd have to go next door to the Glennallen Lodge to use its facilities.

We had to keep track of the time, however, since the lodge closed at midnight. Woe betide us if we had not attended to bodily needs before then, because once the lodge was closed, we were stuck to our own devices until eight or nine the next morning.

McNall claimed to have developed a bodily rhythm matched to that of the lodge. I'm glad he had. As for the rest of us, we tried to avoid staying overnight in the office trailer in the winter. Later, we got rid of the trailer and moved our office into a space in the old Caribou Hotel, which was a lot more convenient and comfortable.

Once the pipeline had been completed, Glennallen settled down somewhat and we found that maintaining an office there was just not feasible. We finally closed our Glennallen office.

We met a lot of wonderful people there, however, and we still get more than our share of clients from Glennallen.

Chapter 33
Blackacre

When I lived in Milwaukee, radio station WGN in Chicago came in loud and clear. During the 1960s a fellow named Franklyn MacCormack had a program called the Meister Brau Showcase from 11:05 PM until 5:30 AM six nights a week. MacCormack had a deep, wonderful voice and he played romantic music and read great poetry.

One of the poems he read regularly was *Vagabond's House* by Don Blanding. *Vagabond's House* is found in a book by the same name. My copy, autographed by Blanding, was printed in 1945 and even back then, the book was in its thirty-fifth printing.

The poem begins:

> When I have a house ... as I sometime may ...
> I'll suit my fancy in every way.
> I'll fill it with things that have caught my eye
> In drifting from Iceland to Molokai ...

The poem describes the dreamer's house in great detail including "all of the corners and all the nooks ... all the bookshelves and all the books" and goes on:

> My house will stand on the side of a hill
> By a slow broad river, deep and still,
> With a tall lone pine on guard nearby
> Where the birds can sing and the stormwinds cry ...

It describes a "fireplace where the fir logs blaze, and the smoke rolls up in a waving haze". The house would have "a shingle loose somewhere, to wail like a banshee in despair, when the wind is high and the storm-gods race, and I am snug by my fireplace".

Vagabond's House is a terrific poem and when read in the wee hours of the night by Franklyn MacCormack, a listener could almost visualize the house.

I vowed that someday I would build such a house.

When Barbara and I were taken to the Anchorage "Hillside" on our first evening in our new town, we fell in love with the view. The Hillside is part of the foothills of the Chugach Mountains. To the west, when it is clear, the full sweep of the Alaska Range is visible even though those

Wayne, Barbara, Gregory, and Brian Ross at their home at 1326 P Street, Anchorage, Alaska (circa 1973).

mountains are a hundred miles away. To the north are the Talkeetnas, twenty to thirty miles away, and to the northwest is Sleeping Lady Mountain, some forty miles away. Finally, on a really clear day Mount Hunter, Mount Foraker, and even Mount McKinley can be seen on the horizon, at a distance of almost two hundred miles!

From the Hillside all of Anchorage is visible, as well as Knik Arm, Turnagain Arm, and Cook Inlet. I firmly believe ninety-eight percent of the people in the world have never seen a view as wonderful as the one from the Anchorage Hillside. We wanted to build a house incorporating that view.

But we couldn't find any affordable land to buy. In 1968 Hillside land was going for $5,000 an acre. We certainly could not afford such an expense.

In the meantime we needed a place to live. Our apartment was just getting too small so we bought a lot close to downtown and built our 1326 P Street duplex, living in the upper unit while renting the lower unit.

One summer there was a large forest fire on the Hillside. We could see the smoke from the front window of our duplex. After the fire was out, we drove up to see the damage. Many acres were blackened but the spectacular view was undiminished. We renewed our vow to live with that view.

Then we heard about an attorney named Bob Hammond who owned some Hillside land. We looked him up in the phone book, set up an appointment, and went to see him. Hammond himself lived on the Hillside. He was only too pleased to take us around and show us what he had for sale.

Bob Hammond told us he had bought 320 acres on the Hillside in 1963 at a cost of $300 an acre. He then had the parcels subdivided, and had roads put in. Since that time, Hammond had stepped back from the practice of law. If he was able to sell four or five parcels of land every year, he made a pretty good living without having to work very hard.

Hammond showed us quite a number of available parcels but there was one lot we liked more than others. It was at 1,350 feet in elevation and a little more than an acre and a half in size. Hammond wanted $24,500 for it. Barbara and I went back home to talk.

Hammond had a $300-per-acre investment which, after subdividing, had jumped to $5,000-per- acre by 1968, when we had visited the Hillside for the first time. A year or two later the price was $9,000 an acre. A year or two after that it was $12,000 an acre. Now, only ten years after his initial purchase, Hammond was asking, and getting, $16,000 an acre. We could see the ever increasing price of Hillside land was going to always be out of our reach. We needed to be creative.

Finally I came up with a plan. I offered Hammond ten percent down. I then proposed we pay only interest payments on the unpaid balance plus $100 each month for the first year. The next year we'd pay interest plus $200 a month. The third year we's pay interest plus $300 a month. Each year we'd pay an additional $100 per month. Finally, we proposed to pay the land off, with a balloon payment, in the seventh year.

Bob Hammond, nice guy that he was, accepted our offer! He said he remembered his days as a young attorney when things were tough, and he knew we wanted that land.

For several years we made our payments regularly, all the while planning the house that we'd build someday.

I'd read *Vagabond's House* and planned "all of the corners and all the nooks, and all the bookshelves and all the books." We'd seen the movie *My Fair Lady* and chose to have a two- story library like that in Professor Higgins' house. We came across a picture in a book which showed what was called a Great Room and we incorporated such a room into our planned house. I put all of our wishes into a floor plan which I drew of the house and we took it to an engineer. From our paperwork he prepared formal building plans.

Now all we needed was a builder.

In 1976 we went back to the Midwest to see our parents. I showed the house plans to my dad.

"I know a great builder!" Dad said. "Gene Ritzer! Gene always talks about the time in 1942 when he worked on building the Alcan Highway. Gene says he'd sure like to go back to Alaska for a visit. If you can get him to build your house, you can be sure it would be done right. I'm going to invite him here for dinner tonight, and you just show him your house plans. Let's see what he says!"

So Dad invited Gene Ritzer to dinner that night. Gene lived in Eagle River, Wisconsin, where Dad had a vacation home. He was what the locals called a "master builder" and was well respected in the building trade.

According to plan, after dinner Dad suggested that Barbara and I show Gene our house plans. After Gene studied them a bit, he asked some questions. Finally he said "Boy! I'd sure like to build that for you!"

"OK!" I said. "We'll see you next summer!"

Gene looked surprised and then a faraway look came into his eyes. "That would be something!" he replied. Nothing more was said.

At 7:00 AM the next morning, the phone rang. The call was for me. It was Gene Ritzer. "Are you serious about wanting me to build your house in Alaska?" he asked.

"I sure am!" I replied.

"Well," said Gene, "I talked to Evelyn (his wife) and she said I can do it provided she comes along."

And that was that. We had a builder!

In preparation for the house, Barbara and I first had to get a well in place to be sure we had water. We lined up a well-driller who was going to charge us $20 per foot.

The owner of the lot next door had gone down 165 feet before he found water so, to be on the safe side, we budgeted for 200 feet. Our well-driller had to go down 432 feet before he struck water! But the water came in at six gallons a minute, which was plenty.

Later I attached a thirty-foot flagpole to the well casing and bragged I had a 462-foot flagpole on our property. I tried to avoid revealing, however, 432 feet of the pole was below ground.

We also installed a septic system.

The following April, Gene drove to Alaska in a new pickup truck which our Girl Friday, Vina Young from Cordova, had ordered. After delivering the new truck to Vina in Cordova, Gene spent several days in Anchorage, walking our land, getting properly licensed, getting insured, and familiarizing himself with what was available for building supplies in Alaska. He also spent time ascertaining any differences in building an Alaska house from one in Wisconsin. Then Gene flew back to Wisconsin.

Right after breakup we hired an excavator to dig the basement. The excavator found bedrock so close to the surface he thought he would have to use dynamite to get the basement in. As it was, he broke three teeth off his backhoe before he got the hole dug properly.

In June 1977, Gene and Evelyn Ritzer arrived in Alaska, ready to build. He brought a full building crew with him consisting of his two brothers-both in their 60s-and their wives, and two of Gene's sons. A third son arrived later with his wife and young child. There was also a friend of Gene's sons, Carl Brent, an 18-year-old guy who was simply looking for adventure.

They had all driven in a caravan from Wisconsin. The caravan had four vehicles, and several campers. Gene said they looked like "Okies moving to California except that our vehicles are newer."

I had hauled the old law office trailer from Glennallen to Anchorage. I set it up on our lot for Gene and Evelyn to live in, and hooked it up to the well and septic system. Gene's brothers set up their campers at a camper park several miles away. Gene's sons and their friend, Carl Brent, moved into tents on the property.

Master Builder Gene Ritzer delivering the keys to Vina Young's new Chevrolet pickup truck in Cordova, Alaska, April 1977.

Then they all went to work. Gene said he and his crew would work six days a week. On the seventh day, Sunday, I was expected to take them fishing. That fishing guide bit was tough duty but I did not object because if somebody had to do it, I figured it might as well be me.

I'd work five to six days at Reasor's law office, and then visit the building site whenever I could, usually in the evenings and on Saturdays. On Sunday I took everybody fishing. It worked out pretty well.

More than once, just when I was in the middle of a meeting with a client, I'd get a phone call. "Hey Wayne! This is Gene. Can you bring us up a box of number nine drop-point, concrete-coated sinker nails? We need some this afternoon."

I didn't even know what number nine drop-point, concrete-coated sinker nails were! But I wrote down what they wanted, picked it up over my lunch hour, and drove it up to the building site.

Gene and his family worked a heavy schedule. Evelyn would have breakfast ready for the crew before 7:00 AM. They'd start "pounding nails" as Gene put it shortly after 7:00 AM, break for ten minutes for coffee and a sweet roll at 9:30, and then go back to work until noon when Evelyn would have lunch ready. They went back to work at 12:30 PM,

On Sundays, the author would have to take Master Builder Gene
Ritzer (left) and Carl Brent (right) and other members of the house
building crew fishing.

worked until 2:30, have a ten minute beer break, and then went back to
work until 5:00 or 5:30 PM. Then Evelyn and the other wives would serve
supper. Some evenings we played Sheepshead[22] or poker but most of the
time Gene's brothers and their wives went back to their campers for the
evening. Gene, however, took advantage of the long daylight hours and
worked until 9:00 or 9:30 PM. Despite those long hours, Gene, who was
paid hourly, refused to charge us for more than eight hours a day.

---

[22] A German card game, famous in Wisconsin (and Bavaria) but seldom played
elsewhere.

Gene and his crew were hard workers. They raised and bolted the beams in the Great Room, by hand, some twenty feet or more in the air. They hand-built an arched front door. They insisted on adding another gable to the house. They noticed from the plans that we had only six and added one more because they wanted to say they built "the house of seven gables" in Alaska. There didn't appear to be anything they couldn't do.

Barbara and the kids and I moved into the house in October 1977.

During construction, I left Reasor's office and opened my own law office, and we also found out that Barbara was expecting our fourth child. It was a busy but exciting time.

Barbara and I came to the conclusion if a marriage can survive the building of a house, it will survive anything. Our marriage had already survived building two houses! I began telling folks, however, that Barbara and I had a crypt installed in the basement of our Hillside house because "we aren't moving again!"

When the house was habitable, Gene and his crew returned to Wisconsin. Only Carl Brent stayed on. He took our old Glennallen office trailer down to a mobile home park, moved into it, and set about to become an Alaska resident. Several years later I was best man and Barbara was maid of honor at Carl's wedding to Debbie, a girl he had met in Anchorage. A year or two after that we became godparents to their son, whom they named Carl Ross Brent. They still live in Alaska and we remain friends to this day.

Gene came back the following summer to finish the trim on the house. On a number of occasions thereafter I went back to Wisconsin for the whitetail deer season and hunted with the Ritzers.

Some neighbors began calling our home "Rapunzel house" because of the rock turret we put on the front. They said it looked like they imagined the tower in the fairy tale.

We, however, called our house "Blackacre." Blackacre was a generic term used in every law school exam to reference any piece of property. Thus, a law exam question might begin: "A sells Blackacre to B." An exam question would then give the facts of the sale and law students had to analyze the transaction. We law students often said, facetiously of course, if we ever got a chance to buy Blackacre we'd do it and hang on to it. That way future law students would not have to answer any further questions about sales of Blackacre.

Wayne, Barbara, Gregory and Brian Ross on the canoe trails near Sterling, Alaska (circa 1975). We used this picture as our as our Christmas picture at Christmas 1975.

We felt the name Blackacre was also appropriate because the ground and trees still showed the effects of the wildfire that had gone through the area several years before.

We still own Blackacre and still marvel at the view. We have "suited our fancy in every way" and "filled it with things that have caught our eye." We love "all of the corners and all the nooks, and all the bookshelves and all the books."

Our house actually stands "on the side of a hill … with a tall lone pine on guard nearby, where the birds can sing and the stormwinds cry … " We do have the "fireplace-two in fact- where the fir logs blaze, and the smoke rolls up in a waving haze …"

And we made sure that there really is "a shingle loose somewhere, that wails like a banshee in despair, when the wind is high and the storm-gods race, and we are snug by our fireplace … "

And we have been happy together in that home for more than thirty-five years.

Did I mention the view?

Chapter 34
Now It Begins

In 1976, as we started plans for eventually building our house on the Hillside, our third son Timothy Leonard arrived. Since it was the year of the United States Bicentennial, I bought Tim a Model 94 Winchester Bicentennial Commemorative rifle. Three sons! Wow! But we still wanted a girl too.

The fall of 1977 was an eventful time. Ed Reasor and I had a disagreement about the way he was handling a case and I realized I wanted to be my own boss. Ed also wanted to get out of the Glennallen and Cordova offices and I enjoyed handling cases in those small communities. So we worked out a deal where I purchased the assets of those offices, and I left Reasor and Associates to open my own practice.

That was a gutsy move because Barbara was pregnant with our fourth child and we were just about to close on our new house. But despite the risks, on 1 October 1977 I opened the law office of Ross & Associates, and never looked back. That same month we moved into our Hillside home.

Amy Katherine arrived in 1978, only nine months later.

I had a wonderful wife, four lovely kids, and a new business to work in that I owned exclusively.

Life was good, and I wondered what further adventures were in store for us here in the Last Frontier. Only time would tell. But so far, it had been a great ride!

When this picture was taken in 1974 of our second son Brian, none of us knew what further adventures were in store for us in the Last Frontier. How could anyone guess that the little guy in the picture with the flowers, for example, would grow up to become a Lieutenant Colonel in the United States Marines?